# Praise for
# GROWING UP MUSLIM

"This is a wonderful book about Islam—knowledgeable, approachable, and inspiring. By telling the simple truth about the strength she gains from her faith, Sumbul Ali-Karamali brings to life how being a better Muslim helps her be a better American."

—EBOO PATEL,
Founder and President of Interfaith Youth Core
and author of *Sacred Ground*

"The perfect guide for the young person trying to figure out what it means to be a Muslim in this day and age." —REZA ASLAN,
author of *No god but God*

"Sensible, accurate, and engaging—a much-needed corrective to ignorance and misinformation about Islam and Muslims."

—KECIA ALI,
Associate Professor of Religion and
Director of Undergraduate Studies,
Department of Religion, Boston University

"The author offers an exceptional introduction to Islam by demonstrating the diversity among Muslim practices and beliefs. As the author demonstrates repeatedly, Muslims share a common set of reference points that they use to orient their attitudes and actions, but they interpret these through various cultural and community lenses, just as Jews and Christians do."

—PETER GOTTSCHALK,
Professor of Religion, Wesleyan University,
and coauthor of *Islamophobia*

# growing up
# MUSLIM

# *growing up*
# MUSLIM

## Understanding Islamic
## Beliefs and Practices

*Sumbul Ali-Karamali*

DELACORTE PRESS

Visit us on the Web! randomhouse.com/teens
Educators and librarians, for a variety of teaching tools,
visit us at randomhouse.com/teachers

*Library of Congress Cataloging-in-Publication Data*
Ali-Karamali, Sumbul.
    Growing up Muslim : understanding Islamic beliefs and practices / Sumbul Ali-
Karamali. — 1st ed.
        p. cm.
    Includes bibliographical references and index.
    ISBN 978-0-385-74095- 1 (hc trade) — ISBN 978-0-375-98977-3 (glb) —
ISBN 978-0-375-98340-5 (ebook) 1. Islam—Juvenile literature. I. Title.
    BP161.3.A385 2012      297—dc23      2011045056

The text of this book is set in 12.5-point Adobe Caslon.
Book design by Vikki Sheatsley

Printed in the United States of America
10  9  8  7  6  5  4  3  2  1
First Edition

*For my children*

# Contents

## Part I
### Muslim Beliefs and Practices
### (or, What It's Like to Grow Up Muslim in California)

# Part II
## When Did Islam Start and How Did It Develop?

# Part III
## Modern Muslim Demographics

*Part I*

# Muslim Beliefs and Practices
# (or, What It's Like to Grow Up Muslim
# in California)

## Chapter 1

## Starting with the Basics:
## What Do Muslims Eat?

If human beings have one thing in common, whether they are from Switzerland or Swaziland, whether they are Aborigines or Aleuts, it's food. It may not be what *makes* us human (after all, reptiles eat food, too), but it certainly often defines how we live. Food was also the only reason I ever had to talk about religion when I was a kid.

Growing up in Southern California, I almost never talked about being Muslim. None of my elementary school classmates talked about religion, and neither did I. After all, who talks about religion at recess? It wasn't relevant to playing on the playground or doing my homework or going to birthday parties. It just never came up.

Except when it came to food.

The only time I ever had to talk about being Muslim in elementary school, or even middle school, was during the occasional birthday party or playdate when the only food available was, for instance, pepperoni pizza. And then I'd have to explain that I couldn't eat the pepperoni pizza because pepperoni was pork and I didn't eat pork because I was Muslim. *Then* I'd have to explain what being Muslim meant.

Once in a while, being Muslim came up in the classroom as well. I remember when, in seventh grade, we began the study of China in my social studies class. One day, a classmate's mother, who had immigrated from China, brought wontons for the class to taste. She had made the wontons herself. She handed me a wonton nestled in the sort of stiff brown paper napkin that seems to be standard in every classroom. I had never tasted wontons, but I liked trying new foods. I saw that this bite-sized object looked like it was made of some type of dough, and I popped it into my mouth.

As I chewed thoughtfully, I heard a classmate ask the mother, "What's inside it?"

"It's pork," she said, passing by my desk.

I froze. Pork? There I sat, with a mouthful of pork? My religion did not allow me to eat pork! I was afraid to chew it, and I was afraid to swallow it. But I couldn't spit it out, either, because that would have been unthinkably, horrendously *rude,* and my parents had always stressed politeness. What could I do? I sat for a few minutes in my chair, my eyes filling with tears and my mouth full of pork, until I finally gave up and swallowed. I spent the rest of the class period terrified that I would throw up.

That night, I couldn't sleep. Finally, I padded out into the living room, where my parents were watching television, and I told them the whole guilty story. My father laughed and told me that God would forgive me.

"Making a mistake is not a sin," he said, "and yes, I know you realized it was pork and you swallowed it anyway. It's over now, and you did your best. Go back to sleep."

Food is just about the most universal of subjects. We welcome people to our houses with food, build our social lives around food, celebrate with food, and obviously cannot survive without food. It stands to reason, then, that religions might have something to say about food as well.

Many religions set down food guidelines. The guidelines are sometimes periodic (like not eating meat on Fridays) and sometimes permanent (like never eating pork). Islam, which is the religion Muslims follow, contains a few guidelines as well.

The Qur'an, which is the Islamic holy book, tells Muslims not to eat pork or drink alcohol. These are the two best-known prohibitions, and many people have heard of them already. But they aren't the only two.

Another Islamic rule prohibits Muslims from eating animals with fangs, so rattlesnake is out for me. (I cannot say that I'm too disappointed.) I remember being served eel at a sushi restaurant once.

"Do eels have fangs?" I asked my companions hopefully.

The Qur'an also tells Muslims not to eat blood. It prohibits Muslims from eating carrion, which is the flesh of an animal that is already dead. In addition, Muslims may not eat scavenging animals, such as vultures, which are animals that eat corpses or carrion.

The idea of eating carrion, such as an animal found dead in the road, does not sound appetizing at all to me! But carrion may well have been appetizing to people who lived in ancient times. The rules prohibiting consumption of carrion were given to Muslims a long time ago (about fourteen hundred years ago), and in those days people were not as knowledgeable about health. They also didn't necessarily get enough to eat, and so an animal already killed on the road, and available free of charge, may have been perfectly acceptable to them.

Muslim rules on food were probably put in place because of health concerns, though Muslims are supposed to follow them whatever the reason. When Islam was born in the seventh century, people did not have refrigeration or the means to sanitize areas that might have been contaminated with harmful bacteria. They didn't even know about germs in those days. Eating unclean or spoiled food could easily have been fatal, especially since medicines were not as advanced and plentiful as they are today. In fact, even today, eating unclean food can be fatal.

Carrion is unhealthy to eat because the meat begins to

decay as soon as the animal dies, especially in a hot climate. The animal also might have died of a disease harmful to human beings. An animal that regularly eats carrion—like a vulture—is considered by Muslims to be unhealthy, too, because it eats food considered unhealthy for humans.

As for pork, the Qur'an may have prohibited it because pigs, which are omnivores, were known to behave like scavengers and eat carrion. A second reason could have been that pork was prone to getting infected with parasites. Interestingly, Judaism, which Islam considers to be a "sibling" religion, also prohibits pork.

You may be wondering if these dietary restrictions are as relevant today as they were over a thousand years ago. After all, we now have refrigeration. We have improved ways of storing and preparing meat. Pork, for example, can be safe to eat if it is cooked properly and the pig has been raised on a farm, on a healthy diet.

In the case of Islam, though, many of these dietary restrictions come from the Qur'an, which Muslims believe is the word of God. Therefore, whatever the reasons for the dietary restrictions, Muslims are still expected to follow them. That doesn't mean all Muslims do follow them—as in any other religion, some people follow the rules and some do not.

I always feel lucky that the abundance of food in my life allows me to make choices about what to eat—choices that other people around the world may not have. When

I was growing up, most people in America ate meat at least once a day. But these days, Americans have all sorts of diets and all sorts of reasons for them.

I did find, growing up, that pork cropped up in the oddest places. Nobody I knew, Muslim or otherwise, ate carrion or scavengers or anything with fangs! But non-Muslims I knew did eat pork. And sometimes they didn't realize that "bacon bits" on top of a spinach salad were pork or that ham and salami and bacon and pepperoni were all pork as well.

I had one teacher who kept telling me that I didn't know what I was missing by not eating bacon. I never really knew what to say to him. Though I liked and respected him, he was the teacher and I was the student.

"What's going to happen to you if you eat pork? Will you get struck down by lightning?" he demanded once.

"I understand that you love bacon," I finally said one day. "I'm sure it's delicious, and I think there's nothing wrong with other people eating it if they want to. But it's just not something *I* eat."

Muslims are allowed to eat any meat that is not specifically forbidden. When I was growing up in Los Angeles, our family ate mostly beef, chicken, and lamb. In India, where my parents spent their childhoods, goat meat is very common.

The meat Muslims are allowed to eat must be *halal*. In Islam, *halal* means "allowed" or "permissible." For meat to be permissible to eat, certain requirements must be met. These requirements were originally developed not only for health considerations, but also to promote more humane practices toward animals.

These are the requirements for meat to be qualified as halal:

- the animal may not be tortured or mistreated while it's alive;
- before it is killed, a prayer must be said over the animal, to show the intention of killing it for food and not for sport;
- the animal's throat must be cut swiftly and with a sharp knife (especially in the seventh century, this was the quickest and most painless way of killing an animal);
- the animal must also be killed outside the presence of other animals;
- and before it can be cooked, the blood must be drained out of it.

In England and Scotland, you can find a type of sausage called "black pudding." It's also called "blood sausage." It's made mostly of blood, mixed with oats or barley, and enhanced with spices. Because of the last halal requirement above, black pudding is not something I, as a Muslim, am allowed to eat.

Sometimes, dietary restrictions arise unexpectedly—as in the case of marshmallows. I love marshmallows. But they do present a potential problem for Muslims.

Marshmallows contain gelatin, which comes from

animals. Sometimes gelatin comes from pigs, and sometimes it comes from cows or horses. The ingredients list on the marshmallow package usually says simply "gelatin." It does not say whether the gelatin came from a pig or from another animal.

My parents came to the United States before there were many Muslims here and before food packages listed ingredients in such detail. I don't think my parents realized, when I was a child, that gelatin might come from a pig, so I was allowed to eat marshmallows!

But some Muslims of my acquaintance did grow up knowing that the gelatin in marshmallows might come from pigs. Even then, they didn't all come to the same conclusions about whether they could eat marshmallows. They still don't.

Some Muslims decided that eating marshmallows was allowable. They reasoned that if they didn't know for *certain* that the gelatin came from a pig, then they were allowed the benefit of the doubt. Or perhaps they decided that even if the gelatin did come from a pig, it was so processed and so tiny an amount that it wasn't really like eating pork.

Other Muslims decided not to eat marshmallows at all. They reasoned that even if the gelatin did not come from a pig, it still came from an animal that had not been prepared according to the Muslim rules of halal butchering. Or perhaps they preferred to stay on the safe side and avoid marshmallows altogether, just in case.

Different Muslims can arrive at different conclusions and still be practicing their religion. But these days, we have a solution to the marshmallow dilemma: we can buy halal marshmallows! These are made with gelatin that comes from a halal animal. I have one friend who never tasted a marshmallow until recently, when I gave her a package of halal marshmallows. She exclaimed, "Now I can make s'mores!"

In fact, I was pleasantly shocked one day when I arrived at the Indian-Pakistani grocery store nearby and nearly bumped into a showy display of "Halal Krispy Treats." I couldn't help laughing. They were just like Rice Krispies Treats but were made with halal marshmallows. I could picture the manufacturers of halal marshmallows as Muslim kids growing up in America, dying to taste Rice Krispies Treats (but not allowed to) and waiting impatiently to become adults so that they could develop their own halal version!

The other option for Muslims is to buy vegan marshmallows. They are made without any animal products. I actually like these the best.

Marshmallows aside, sometimes eating meat in restaurants or in other people's houses can be problematic for Muslims. This is because of the halal butchering requirement. Meat in restaurants or in non-Muslim households is very unlikely to be butchered according to halal standards (except in Muslim-majority countries). For this reason, while I was growing up, a few Muslims I knew did not eat meat in restaurants at all. But most Muslims I knew *were* comfortable eating meat at McDonald's or at their neighborhood pizza parlors.

The Muslims (including my own family) who ate meat in restaurants thought it was allowable for one or more reasons. First, perhaps they did not strictly observe the rules of halal butchering and were not particular as to whether they ate halal or not. Not all Muslims are strictly observant. My Jewish friends had similar issues in their families—some ate only food prepared according to kosher laws, but some did not. Second, they may have been relying on a verse of the Qur'an that says that Muslims are allowed to eat the food of Jews and Christians (except specifically forbidden foods like pork). Since the United States is a predominantly Christian country, some Muslims concluded that food in restaurants was the food of Jews and Christians and therefore allowable for them to eat. Muslims considered kosher food to be allowable for them, too. I grew up eating a lot of all-beef kosher hot dogs at Dodger Stadium in Los Angeles. Third, they may have decided that eating non-halal meat was acceptable if there was no alternative. When I was growing up, even finding vegetarian food was not always easy. At times, the choice came down to either eating non-halal meat or not eating at all. Different Muslims chose differently.

In my immediate family, we follow the Qur'anic verse that allows Muslims the food of Jews and Christians; therefore, we are not too particular about our meat being butchered according to halal butchering standards. However, there's another restriction that we *are* particular about: in Islam, animals are not supposed to be tortured or mistreated. Because of this, and for reasons of compassion, I eat only meat from animals that have been humanely raised and slaughtered. This is my personal choice on how to follow my religion, and other Muslims may disagree.

Besides laying out meat-related prohibitions, the Qur'an, as interpreted by nearly all Muslims, prohibits alcohol and anything else that *intoxicates*. That's why recreational drugs, and not just alcoholic drinks, are disallowed for Muslims. Here's an exception, though: if a Muslim needs a drug for serious medical reasons, Islam allows it, even if it may cause intoxication.

Adult social situations sometimes involve alcohol, and Muslims may feel awkward if they cannot drink it. My father first came to California from India to earn his doctorate, because he wanted to be a university professor. While in graduate school, he found that all his friends (none of them Muslim) drank beer. They couldn't believe he had never tried it. But he simply smiled and shook his head when someone offered it to him.

When my father began teaching mathematics in college, sometimes he and my mother held parties for his math department colleagues and their spouses. I remember that my mother would make dinner for fifty people, including a hundred Indian *chapati* (breads that look like tortillas but are stretchier), all stacked a foot high in a perfect cylinder on a plate. My parents' American friends loved Indian food; the problem for my parents was that their friends and colleagues liked alcohol at parties, too.

Muslims are not only supposed to refrain from

drinking alcohol, they are also supposed to refrain from offering it to others. The reason is that if you think something is harmful for you, then you should not lead others to harm themselves with it. However, this put my parents in a quandary: their very strong sense of hospitality (the idea that their guests should be made comfortable and happy) warred with their sense that they shouldn't offer something they wouldn't drink themselves.

Which side won? Their sense of hospitality.

"My friend will drink alcohol whether I buy it for him or not," said my father. "He will simply leave my party and go out and buy his own wine if I don't have it here for him, and, as a host, I cannot let him do it. I will buy it for him, and when he comes here, he can drink it."

Alcohol pops up unexpectedly in desserts and candies, too. In college, one of my friends, an American whose parents lived in Germany, sometimes brought me mouth-watering chocolates when she came back from Munich. They were individually wrapped and the ingredients were not listed. I didn't worry about what the ingredients might be, because Islam has no prohibition against chocolate (thank goodness). Years later, though, another friend brought me a whole box of the same German chocolates.

"I got these for you," she said, "and I figured you wouldn't mind that they have brandy in them."

Brandy? Alcohol? My heart sank.

"Oh, no!" I said, smiling ruefully. "Why did you have to tell me that they contain alcohol? Now I can't ever eat them again!"

I must point out that some Muslims would consider this amount of alcohol—such a small amount in a small candy—to be acceptable and not something to worry about. But other Muslims say that even a small amount of alcohol is not acceptable. I understand both views and accept them, but in my personal life I am most comfortable staying away from even tiny amounts of alcohol. I sadly said goodbye forever to my favorite chocolates.

All these Islamic food rules are subject to an important exception: if someone is starving to death or there's extreme necessity, then he or she can eat even food that is normally prohibited. In Islam, preservation of life is paramount, and if breaking a food restriction is necessary to preserve life, then it's allowable for that particular situation.

Religious dietary restrictions, therefore, like other aspects of religion, do not always draw clear lines as to what's allowed and what's not allowed. People can come up with different interpretations of the general rules. And even devout people who believe strongly in their religion may not choose to follow every traditional religious rule. In this way, Muslims are just as diverse as people of other religions.

*Chapter 2*

## Definitions and the Declaration of Faith

Human beings assign many names to God, depending upon the language and the tradition. For example, the French word for God is "Dieu." The Spanish word is "Dios." The Persian word is "Khuda." The Arabic word is "Allah."

"Allah" simply means "God" or "the God." "Allah" does not mean "Exclusively Islamic God" or "the Only Valid God in the World." It just means "God." In fact, Arabic-speaking Jews and Christians have historically called their God Allah. Some Malaysian Christians, too, have begun using "Allah" to refer to God.

From time to time, I hear someone say, "Muslims

worship Allah." That's like saying "Mexicans worship Dios." We would normally say that Mexicans worship God. In the same way, we ought to say that Muslims worship God. Otherwise, the implication is that Muslims worship an entity other than God.

The word "Muslim" means "someone who submits to God." What's the difference between "Muslim" and "Islam"? "Islam" is the name of the religion, and a Muslim is someone who believes in Islam—just as "Christianity" is the name of a religion, and a Christian is someone who believes in Christianity.

It is easier to understand the words "Islam" and "Muslim" if you consider how root words work. Perhaps you have learned some Greek or Latin roots in school. You may know that roots are groups of letters from which words are built. For example, "cycl" means "wheel," from which we get the words "bicycle" (two wheels) and "tricycle" (three wheels).

Both of the Arabic words "Islam" and "Muslim" originate from the same Arabic root. You can spot the letters common to both. The Arabic root for both words is a group of three letters with the sounds *s-l-m*. This root means "to be in peace."

The word "Islam," then, comes from the root that means "to be in peace." That's why the word "Islam" itself means both "submission to God" and "peace." Putting those together, "Islam" means "submitting to God's peace" or "the peace that comes from submission to God." One

Muslim scholar translates Islam as "entering into God's peace." It never, ever means "submitting or surrendering to another person." Only to God.

A "Muslim" is someone who "submits to God and finds peace" or "enters into God's peace." Therefore, a Muslim is someone who follows the religion of Islam.

Both "Islam" and "Muslim" have adjective forms as well, and these can also be confusing. For example, which term is accurate: "Islamic prayer" or "Muslim prayer"? A "Muslim holiday" or an "Islamic holiday"? Generally, the adjective "Islamic" relates to the religion of Islam itself, and the adjective "Muslim" relates to the people who follow Islam. Therefore, it is correct to talk about "Muslim students" but not "Islamic students." It is more appropriate to say, for example, "Muslim kids at school" rather than "Islamic kids at school." But you might say "the Islamic rules of prayer" rather than "the Muslim rules of prayer."

The two words overlap in meaning, though, and sometimes it is difficult to tell which should be used. For example, "Muslim scholars" means scholars who are Muslim. But "Islamic scholars" means scholars who study Islam. In my opinion, when in doubt, you should go with "Muslim."

Part of the reason all this can be confusing is that Arabic is hard to translate into English. Its structure is completely different from that of English. The word "Islam" takes in all the following concepts: free acceptance, God, and peace. I have never found an equivalent word in English that contains all of these meanings in one.

"Islam" is an Arabic word because the Prophet of Islam, Muhammad, happened to speak Arabic. He began to preach Islam in seventh-century Arabia. Muslims believe that Muhammad received God's words in the form of verses. These verses were eventually written down into a book called the Qur'an, which is the Islamic holy book, just like the Bible is the Christian holy book. (The Qur'an is discussed in Chapter 13.)

Since Muhammad spoke Arabic, the Qur'an is in Arabic. Muslims pray in Arabic because, during the prayer, they recite verses from the Qur'an. And that's why Muslims often call God "Allah": they are used to praying in Arabic, and "Allah" means "God" in Arabic. But Muslims do not have to call God "Allah" when they're speaking, for example, English.

The only real requirement for being Muslim is belief in God and belief in Muhammad as the Prophet of God. Muslims sum up this belief in the sentence "There is no god but God, and Muhammad is the Messenger of God."

This sentence is called the "Declaration of Faith." It is one of the *Five Pillars of Islam*—that is, one of the five main tenets of the religion. All Muslims agree on the Five Pillars and all Muslims should observe them. The Declaration of Faith is, in some ways, the first and most important one, because if someone recites the Declaration of Faith and believes in it, then that person is a Muslim. The opposite is not true: if someone fasts and prays and follows the other pillars of Islam, but does not believe in the Declaration of Faith, then that person is not considered a Muslim. In Arabic, the Declaration of Faith is called the *shahada*.

Consider the words of the translation "There is no god but God, and Muhammad is the messenger of God." The lowercase "god" refers to a god that is one of many gods or deities. In contrast, the uppercase "God" refers to a single, supreme being. Islam was born in a society where many people worshiped multiple deities or objects from nature. The Declaration of Faith makes the distinction between "God," the single entity, and the various other deities that people at the time worshiped. Therefore, the phrase "There is no god but God" means "There is nothing worthy of worship except for God."

The second part of the Declaration of Faith, the phrase "Muhammad is the Messenger of God," is important, too. It means that Muslims believe Muhammad was chosen by God to deliver God's message to the human beings around him. That is why Muslims consider him a messenger.

Muslims believe that God is neither a "he" nor a "she," but a different kind of entity entirely.

Finally, this phrase clarifies that Muhammad was not divine. He was an important messenger to Muslims, but human. Muslims do not view him as an angel or other immortal being.

Muhammad preached many messages, but perhaps

his main message was belief in one God. Thousands of
years before Muhammad, a man named Abraham had
also preached belief in one God. Muhammad saw himself as continuing the religion of the Prophet Abraham.

Abraham appears in the Jewish and Christian religions, as well as in Islam. Abraham had two sons, Isaac
and Ismail (or Ishmael). Muslims believe that Ismail's
descendants eventually became Muslims, and that Isaac's
descendants eventually became Jews and Christians. That
is why these three religions are called the *Abrahamic* religions. I think of them as sibling religions. Abraham's
message of belief in one God is what is reiterated in the
Declaration of Faith.

Whenever Muslims mention the name of Muham-
mad, the Prophet of Islam, they say, "peace be upon him."
They also add "peace be upon him" whenever they mention the names of Jesus and Moses, who are also considered prophets of Islam, and other prophets. In this text, I
have omitted this phrase for simplicity's sake. I mean no
disrespect; if you are Muslim, please just say the words to
yourself, as I do.

*Chapter 3*

## How Many Times a Day Do You Pray?

Prayer is one of the Five Pillars of Islam, so it's serious business. Muslims are supposed to pray five times every day. The prayer times are spaced out during the day: morning, early afternoon, late afternoon, sunset, and evening.

Prayer of some kind is common to most religions. It may take various forms, but most people understand the basic idea of prayer. Generally, it describes a communication with a deity or other object of worship. It often involves a *supplication,* which is a request or an entreaty.

Muslims pray to God. When I am speaking English, I often mutter "Thank God!" if something goes right for me. But if I am speaking Urdu or Arabic, as when I'm reciting the prayer words, I might say *"Al-Hamdu Lillah,"* which means "Thank God" in everyday usage. (Literally, it means "Praise be to God.") Whichever words I use, I thank the same God every time. I'm in company with Arabic-speaking Jews and Christians, who also use *"Al-Hamdu Lillah."*

Praying five times a day sounds, to most people, like a lot. My friends in school used to ask me, "What do you find to pray about so many times a day?"

Like anybody else, I've prayed for all sorts of things, from the abstract (like health and happiness) to the concrete (like an A on my math test). Once, in sixth grade, I had to give an oral report on a current event of my choice. I did not mind current events, but I was *terrified* of oral reports. I prepared my speech and then prayed every night that the teacher would forget about my report and automatically give me an A without my having to get up in front of the whole class and fall down in a fit of stage fright. My prayer was not answered; I did indeed have to give my report. (Luckily, I didn't fall down.)

The Islamic prayer is more than a supplication, though, more than a request or entreaty. It is also a form of worship—that is, a form of paying respect to God. Therefore, the prayer is composed of two parts: a *recitation,* which is the worshiping section; and a *supplication.* The supplication portion can include giving thanks, not simply asking for help. I think of the recitation portion as a way to give my respect to God and the supplication portion as a time to have a private conversation with God.

In the recitation section, Muslims recite Arabic verses from the Qur'an. These verses are recited in a specific order. Muslims must also follow a structured pattern of standing, kneeling, and bowing when they're praying.

The recitation section concludes with a small gesture that I've always found charming. Muslims must look to the right and say, *"As-salamu Alaykum wa Rahmatullah,"* which means "Peace and the mercy of God be upon you," and then they must look to the left and say the same thing. But who is the "you" in the sentence "Peace and the mercy of God be upon you"? Who are Muslims talking to when they say this?

It's angels! Muslims are talking to angels.

In Muslim tradition, it is said that when we look to the right and then the left, we greet each of our two recording angels with the words "Peace and the mercy of God be upon you." Muslims believe that two recording angels are assigned to each of us to record our good deeds and bad deeds.

At the end of the recitation section is the time for the supplication, or the personal conversation with God. This is where Muslims can ask for help or thank God for their blessings or say just about anything at all. The supplication may be in any language. Mine is in English or Urdu or both, depending on how I feel. The supplication is also called the *du'a*.

When my friends asked me what I prayed for five

times a day, I replied that sometimes I did not pray for anything at all. Sometimes I performed only the required recitation section and did not make any supplication, which is optional.

Once Muslims have begun to pray one of the daily prayers, they may not interrupt that particular prayer or stop praying until they reach the end of it, when they greet both their recording angels. For example, if I start praying the noon prayer, I cannot speak to anyone or look around or take a break until I come to the end of the prayer, when I look to my right and to my left. "Breaking" a prayer like this would be considered disrespectful to God. The exception, though, is in the case of an emergency.

"You mean an emergency like if a cobra leaps onto your prayer rug and rears back its head so it can sink its fangs into you?" I asked my mother when I was eight years old.

"Well, yes," replied my mother, doubtfully but politely, "but I was actually thinking about, say, a child about to walk into danger or hurt itself. You could break your prayer to prevent the child from being hurt."

I shrugged. The cobra seemed more likely to me.

Because the Islamic prayer involves bending, kneeling, touching the forehead to the ground, sitting up, repeating the whole sequence, and then looking to the right and to the left, it can be fairly conspicuous! It is not easy to accomplish in public without anyone noticing.

When I was in middle school, I attended a "Sunday

school" that was mostly a group of my parents' friends and acquaintances who met in a garage to teach us the basics of our religion. I remember when my Sunday school teacher, a rather stern friend of my father's, asked us, "What would you do if you were working at a job and it was time to pray?"

We all squirmed on our folding chairs. I dreaded the thought of having to pray while others stared at me. And we were in *middle school,* a time when it's not always easy to be different.

"What you would do," my Sunday school teacher continued firmly, "is pray when it was time to pray."

"Yeah, and they'll think I'm a total alien," I thought, rolling my eyes.

"I pray in my office," he continued, "and I've explained it to my colleagues. If they come in and see me praying, they come back later."

I listened politely, but I had serious doubts. I was the only Indian in my middle school class, which meant I was already different. Most people want to fit in with friends and peers, and I was no exception. My fellow middle school students were sometimes painfully concerned with superficial appearances of all kinds, whether these involved race, religion, height (or, as in my case, lack of it), clothing, orthodontics, or glasses.

Luckily, praying in front of others was not an issue I had to confront in middle school or high school, because my school schedule usually allowed me to be at home for my prayers. If I did miss a prayer because of a school event, I "made it up" later—that is, I prayed it later, when I got the chance.

Praying on time is required, though, and Muslims are supposed to pray during the recommended times. Muslims who are too ill or infirm to bend and kneel can pray sitting down or even lying down. So, according to Islamic requirements, I should have tried to pray at school if it meant missing a prayer otherwise.

But at a time when few had heard of Islam and almost nobody understood what Muslims believed and practiced, it was too hard for me to be so conspicuous. My personal decision was to make up my prayer later if I missed it. Other Muslims might have made a different personal decision. That's an example of the difference between what Islam says that Muslims should do and what Muslims do. Religion gives us guidelines, but how to implement the guidelines is up to individuals.

Some students do make arrangements with their teachers or school administrators to take a break during the school day and go to a private place to pray. I know a Muslim who carries a prayer rug wherever he goes. He simply finds a quiet corner in which to pray, whether it is private or not.

A prayer rug is not required for prayer. All that is required is a clean place. That's why mosques require that people remove their shoes before they enter the prayer area; it's important to keep the carpets clean. Carrying a prayer rug simply ensures having a clean place to pray.

When I was young, prayer rugs were not available, so

we prayed on sheets. Now I own several small, colorful
prayer rugs, each just large enough for one person to pray
on. I confess that I prefer them to sheets, because they're
convenient and soft, which makes them more comfortable for kneeling.

But why do Muslims pray so much during the day?
Five daily prayers sounds excessive to many people. Part
of the answer lies in the following story. It comes from
the Islamic religious tradition, which consists of the historical religious writings of Muslim scholars. This is my
version of the Islamic story of why Muslims pray five
times a day:

Imagine a man asleep, oblivious of the wind whispering across the desert city where he has lived all his life.
He is bearded, like the other men of his time and culture,
and though he looks strong, the lines in his face attest to
grief and exhaustion. He does not lie comfortably in his
bed, but has fallen deeply asleep on the ground, near the
ancient cubical building where he has been praying for
many hours. His beloved wife of nearly twenty-five years
has died recently, and he has not yet recovered from the
pain of her loss. The year is sometime around 620 and he
is about fifty years old.

As the man dreams, an angel materializes next to him
and touches his shoulder. The man does not wake. The
angel takes the man's shoulder more firmly and shakes
him, but the man continues to sleep. Perhaps a small line
of exasperation appears on the angel's brow as the angel

tries to awaken the man for the third time, possibly calling his name: "Muhammad! Awake!"

Muhammad, the Prophet of Islam, lifts heavy eyelids to behold the angel Gabriel, an incongruously brilliant sight against the muted gold desert backdrop. He pulls himself wearily to his feet and follows the angel, only to widen his eyes when he sees before him, unbelievably, a creature resembling a winged horse. He mounts the horse with not a little bemusement and flies off into the inky night sky with the angel Gabriel. They soar through the star-studded darkness (this was before smog) and eventually descend to the legendary city of Jerusalem, where Muhammad finds a group of men waiting for him. These men have names from the Torah, the Bible, and the Qur'an—Moses, Abraham, Jesus—and they are all, Muslims believe, prophets of God who lived and preached before Muhammad was born.

There on Temple Mount in Jerusalem, according to the story, Muhammad and the prophets pray together. Afterward, he and the angel Gabriel travel through seven heavens, where they see other angels and meet the other prophets again. They travel even further, to Paradise, where Muhammad is brought, trembling and awestruck, into the presence of God.

It's at this point that God tells Muhammad that he and his followers must pray fifty times a day. That's right, *fifty*. I figure that comes out to about once every fifteen or twenty minutes, depending on how much you sleep.

As Muhammad exits from God's presence, he meets Moses, who asks for a summary of the visit, but then stops in his tracks to say, incredulously, "Fifty? Fifty times a *day*? Your followers will *never* be able to pray fifty times a day! Ask for a reduction."

Muhammad nervously does as Moses suggests, and God reduces the required number of prayers a day to forty.

When Moses hears about this, he (I imagine) clutches his hair in frustration.

"Are you out of your *mind*?" he demands. "I *know* these people! I used to *live* with them! They'll never pray forty times a day! Go back and ask for another reduction."

So God reduces the number of required prayers a day to thirty.

Moses probably buries his face in his hands in frustration. He sends Muhammad back. God reduces the number to twenty. Moses loses patience. Muhammad reluctantly returns. The number is reduced to ten, and then, finally, five.

"You're going to have an uphill battle, getting them to pray five times a day, mark my words," comments Moses resignedly, shaking his head. But Muhammad, ashamed, refuses to plead any further. (I have always wondered if God was just teasing.)

That's the Islamic story of how Muhammad was told to pray five times a day. Five daily prayers are really not so difficult to do, compared to fifty! Each required prayer takes around five minutes to complete. A friend of mine meditates three times a day, and I think of prayer as somewhat similar to meditation. For me, it is a way to stop what I'm doing, slow down, and re-center myself.

Muslims pray during windows of time. The day is divided into five windows, essentially as follows: between dawn and sunrise (Fajr); early afternoon (Zuhr); late afternoon (Asr); sunset (Maghrib); and night (Isha). The exact times of the windows change according to the seasons and the length of the days. If you live close to or on the equator, then the length of the days does not vary much at all. Days and nights at the equator last just about twelve hours each, all year long. The farther you are from the equator, the more the length of the days and nights varies.

For example, in Seattle, Washington, the prayer times vary considerably throughout the year. During the winter, prayer windows shorten because the day is shorter; in the summer, prayer windows are longer because the day is longer. The following is a sample of what prayer times in Seattle usually look like in June:

| | FAJR | (Sunrise) | ZUHR | ASR | MAGHRIB | ISHA |
|---|---|---|---|---|---|---|
| JUNE 15 | 2:58 AM | 5:11 AM | 1:15 PM | 6:38 PM | 9:10 PM | 11:21 PM |
| JUNE 16 | 2:58 AM | 5:11 AM | 1:15 PM | 6:38 PM | 9:10 PM | 11:22 PM |
| JUNE 17 | 2:58 AM | 5:11 AM | 1:15 PM | 6:39 PM | 9:11 PM | 11:22 PM |
| JUNE 18 | 2:57 AM | 5:11 AM | 1:16 PM | 6:39 PM | 9:11 PM | 11:23 PM |
| JUNE 19 | 2:57 AM | 5:11 AM | 1:16 PM | 6:39 PM | 9:11 PM | 11:23 PM |
| JUNE 20 | 2:57 AM | 5:12 AM | 1:16 PM | 6:40 PM | 9:11 PM | 11:23 PM |

The time for the dawn prayer begins at Fajr and ends at sunrise. The time for the early-afternoon prayer (the

Zuhr prayer) begins at Zuhr and ends at Asr. For example, on June 15, a Muslim could pray the Zuhr prayer between 1:15 and 6:38 p.m. The times are quite different in the winter, as shown in the following sample of prayer times for December in Seattle:

|  | FAJR | (Sunrise) | ZUHR | ASR | MAGHRIB | ISHA |
|---|---|---|---|---|---|---|
| DEC. 15 | 6:15 AM | 7:51 AM | 12:09 PM | 2:34 PM | 4:20 PM | 5:53 PM |
| DEC. 16 | 6:16 AM | 7:51 AM | 12:10 PM | 2:35 PM | 4:20 PM | 5:53 PM |
| DEC. 17 | 6:17 AM | 7:52 AM | 12:10 PM | 2:35 PM | 4:20 PM | 5:53 PM |
| DEC. 18 | 6:17 AM | 7:53 AM | 12:11 PM | 2:35 PM | 4:21 PM | 5:54 PM |
| DEC. 19 | 6:18 AM | 7:53 AM | 12:11 PM | 2:36 PM | 4:21 PM | 5:54 PM |
| DEC. 20 | 6:19 AM | 7:54 AM | 12:12 PM | 2:36 PM | 4:21 PM | 5:54 PM |

I always find it easier to pray during the summer, because the windows of time do not rush by so quickly.

Both men and women should dress modestly when they pray. Women cover their hair for the prayer, and men may wear a cap. Men must cover themselves from the knees up, so they generally wear long pants. During the prayer, most women wear clothing that covers everything but their hands, face, and feet, but any clothing that accomplishes this is acceptable. Historically some Muslim women prayed with their heads uncovered, but these days women cover their hair when praying. There's more information on what Muslims wear in Chapter 9.

A friend of mine asked me once why I thought hair was a bad thing. She knew I covered it during prayer. At the time, I had hair so long I could sit on it, which was fun (though inconvenient), so I certainly didn't think of it as *bad*. The reason Muslims cover their hair is to show respect in the presence of God. When Muslims pray, we are communicating with God, and we feel the need to be respectful. Although respect may be shown in any number of ways, covering the hair or head has always been one way, throughout history and in many cultures.

For example, I know several Catholic women who grew up covering their hair in church. Some of my family's Jewish friends also covered their hair when attending synagogue, though they did not cover their hair otherwise. And Sikh women commonly cover their heads when they enter their temples. The reason is the same: respect.

Just as Jews may attend synagogues or Christians may attend churches, Muslims may attend mosques. The English word "mosque" comes from the Arabic word *masjid*, which means a "place of prayer." The mosque is where Muslims can go to pray in a group.

When Muslims pray in a group, one person leads the prayer. He or she is like the conductor of an orchestra. He recites aloud the elements of the prayer, and the rest follow along, bending and kneeling in unison. The one leading the prayer should be the most learned person of the group, but he is not necessarily a religious authority.

This person leading the prayer is generally referred to as an *imam*. You might hear people refer to him as "the imam for this prayer" rather than "the imam," because often the person leading the prayer is not a religious scholar, but simply someone leading that prayer that day or in that group or in that mosque. The person who led our prayer in the two-car garage that served as our mosque was an accountant.

However, the word "imam" can also mean someone who *is* a religious scholar, and not just a prayer leader. (For the Shi'a it means something different still, as explained in Chapter 15.) Other words also may describe religious scholars, such as *shaykh, mufti, maulvi,* and *mullah.* But there is no standardized worldwide procedure for learning enough to be a shaykh; this means, unfortunately, that people could adopt these titles even though they have very little religious education or even none at all. So if you hear someone referred to as an "imam" or a "shaykh," he may be learned and educated in Islam, or he may not be.

Usually, men and women pray in separate lines. The reason for this is that Muslims stand very close together while praying. For some people, at least, standing shoulder to shoulder with someone of the opposite sex might be distracting. Sometimes the lines are tight and we are somewhat squished together! The traditional Muslim reasoning is that it would be difficult to focus on God in prayer when you're squished against someone of the opposite sex.

Can a woman be an imam and lead the prayer? In Islam, women have long been accepted as muftis (Islamic religious scholars). In addition, even in early Islam, women were allowed to be judges, or *qadis.* But whether women can also lead the prayer in a mixed-gender congregation is a question that Muslims are currently debating.

Women have always been allowed to lead a group of females in prayer. But traditionally, when the congregation of Muslims contains both males and females, a man leads the prayer. Some Muslims today believe that women should be allowed to lead the prayer even if men are praying in the group, but others believe that only men can lead mixed-gender prayers.

The most common reason cited for not allowing women to lead a mixed-gender prayer is modesty. That's why women and men pray in separate lines. Usually, the women stand in the back, because (the argument goes) men would be distracted by looking at women's bodies. In addition, some people object to women-led prayer simply because it is not traditional.

At least one respected modern scholar says that a woman can lead a mixed-gender prayer if she does not stand directly in front of the men. Women could stand on the right side of the room, men could stand on the left side of the room, and the woman leading the prayer could stand on the right, in front of the women, but leading the whole congregation. Or, as another scholar suggests, the men could be in a different room from the women, and the woman leading the prayer could be heard over a sound system.

This is the kind of dispute that is not uncommon in religion. Many religions, including Islam, are ancient, and people can disagree on how ancient religious rules should be applied in the modern world. This debate about who can lead the prayer in Islam is similar to the debate in the Catholic church about whether women can become priests; although women have traditionally been banned from becoming Catholic priests, some within the church now challenge this restriction.

Islamic congregational prayers are usually held in mosques, but this is not required. Often, in the United States, the mosques are too small or too few to accommodate all the Muslims who want to attend. That is why holiday prayers are sometimes held elsewhere, such as in parks (with sheets spread on the grass), county fairgrounds, hotel conference rooms, and convention centers.

Most of the mosques in the United States were not originally built as mosques. Rather, they started out as office buildings or community centers or other buildings that Muslims bought and began to use for prayers. As a result, most of the mosques I've attended are singularly unattractive! The church at my university was gorgeous with sparkling mosaic tiles, jewel-like stained glass, and intricate wall carvings that begged to be touched. In contrast, the mosque I attended during high school boasted a few forlorn travel posters randomly tacked to its graying walls.

A mosque need not conform to any particular architectural form. It may be massive and intricate, like the sixteenth-century mosque of Suleiman the Magnificent in Istanbul, Turkey, or it may be a few dozen people meeting in a garage (that would have been me and a group of family acquaintances). In Muslim-majority countries, though, mosques are often spectacular. They are magnificent for the same reason that churches are magnificent— because of a desire on the part of their builders to reflect the glory of God.

Traditionally, the great mosques in Muslim countries were not just places to pray, but were more like community centers, with schools, libraries, hospitals, and gathering places. Every neighborhood had its own, smaller mosque, too, which was essentially just a prayer space for those in the neighborhood to duck into when it was time to pray.

In the United States, mosques are open to non-Muslims as well as Muslims. Most mosques around the world are also open to non-Muslims, though they may close during congregational prayers. In some countries, however, non-Muslims are not allowed into mosques. This is a cultural exclusion, not an Islamic one. The vast majority of Islamic scholars allow non-Muslims to visit mosques.

When my husband traveled to Mali, he went to visit a centuries-old mosque there. He was told that he could not enter the mosque.

"But I'm Muslim, and I'd like to go in," he said.

The guard shook his head and told him that he could not enter the mosque because he was not black! This is clearly a misguided cultural prejudice, because the Prophet Muhammad was not black, either.

The weekly congregational prayer for Muslims is held in the early afternoon on Fridays. Of course, people congregate and pray at other times, too, but the Friday prayer is especially important. Friday is not a day of rest for Muslims, although in some Muslim-majority countries it is a day off from work.

When I was in elementary school, I read too many books featuring supernatural events occurring on Friday the thirteenth. I began to get spooked. When I finally confessed my fears to my mother, she told me that God made *all* the days, so it was illogical to think that some days were cursed. Fridays in particular were special, she added, because Friday was the day of the Muslim congregational prayer.

If you happen to be visiting a country in which Muslims reside, you may hear the "call to prayer," which informs Muslims that it's time to pray. In countries where most of the population is Muslim, the call to prayer is often made through a public address system so that Muslims in the neighborhood can take a break from what they're doing and head to the nearest mosque.

My parents grew up in India, which is not a Muslim-majority country but is home to one of the largest Muslim populations in the world (amounting to 10 to 15 percent of India's total population). The call to prayer can be heard in India, at least in certain places. I have a friend who is an Indian Hindu, and he says he grew up hearing it. He thinks of it as part of his upbringing; though he is not Muslim, he always considered the call to prayer as simply part of the Indian landscape and evidence of a multi-religious society. It is similar to hearing church bells—even for those Indians who are not Christian, church bells are an accepted part of the cultural landscape, too.

Still, in most countries where Muslims are not in the majority, such as in the United States, the call to prayer cannot be heard publicly. It resonates only in the room or building where the congregational prayer is about to begin. It is a signal that the group prayer is about to start and that the people should get into their prayer lines and stop talking.

But what are the words of the call to prayer? In the days of the Prophet Muhammad, Muslims lacked microphones or electricity, so someone would go to a high place and (very loudly) call out these words:

*God is great.*
*God is great.*
*I testify that there is no god but God.*
*I testify that Muhammad is the Messenger of God.*
*Arise and pray!*
*Arise and flourish!*
*God is great.*
*God is great.*
*There is no god but God.*

The call to prayer is in Arabic, not in the English words above. But this is what the words mean in English. The word "great" in this context does not mean great as in "fabulous," as much as it means all-knowing and all-powerful and generally too big for us to comprehend fully. It is said in praise and gratitude and as a request for guidance.

The very first call to prayer took place in the time of the Prophet Muhammad. When Muhammad's followers asked him to select someone to make that first call to prayer—a very great honor—Muhammad chose a Muslim named Bilal. He was not an Arab, but a freed African slave who had joined Muhammad's followers. Bilal was the first *muezzin*, the person who calls people to prayer.

Because the muezzin had to project his voice over quite a distance, he usually stood in an elevated place so that his voice could be heard over the tops of houses and buildings and hills. Searching for a high place near the mosque wasn't always practical, so Muslims began to build slender towers attached to their mosques. These towers are known as *minarets*. The muezzins would climb to the top of the minaret and give the call to prayer from there.

My great-grandfather was the muezzin in his neighborhood mosque in North India. Such was the strength of his voice that people nearly two miles away routinely heard his call to prayer and came in answer. At dawn, when the air was still and quiet, his voice could be heard nearly three miles away.

The call to prayer can be very musical, as it is chanted, not spoken. The Qur'an, as well, is traditionally chanted. It reminds me somewhat of Gregorian chanting in the Christian tradition. Qur'an chanting is a form of art and expertise, and there are rules that one must learn in order to chant properly. In some countries, Qur'an-chanting competitions are held in packed football stadiums!

Before praying, Muslims must wash themselves so that they are clean and respectful before God. Muslims perform a particular ritual of washing before each prayer. It involves washing the hands, face, and feet in a certain order.

And finally, all Muslims face in one particular direction when they pray. Remember my story of the Prophet Muhammad's Night Journey, when he fell asleep near the ancient cubical building in which he had been praying? This cubical building is called the Ka'ba. It is located in Mecca, in Saudi Arabia, and it has been a place of worship for thousands of years. (The Ka'ba is discussed in later chapters.) When Muslims pray, they face the general direction of the Ka'ba.

The Islamic form of prayer, as well as all the rituals attached to it, may look and sound strange and confusing at first. But it is just another way of doing what many people around the world do in many different forms. Some people pray regularly and some do not pray at all, but most of us understand the concept.

*Chapter 4*

# Fasting: The Ultimate Internal Conflict

If food is the one thing that we all have in common, then *lack* of food is certainly something we know we would suffer from. Why, then, would people deprive themselves of food on purpose? It might sound nonsensical. But this is exactly what Muslims do.

During the Islamic month of Ramadan, Muslims deprive themselves of food and water during daylight hours. For the whole month. That's twenty-nine or thirty days of no eating or drinking from dawn (when the horizon begins to lighten, about ninety minutes before sunrise) to sunset.[1] It's called *fasting*.

When I was growing up in California, fasting never came up until late middle school or high school, because kids are not required to fast. But when I began to fast regularly, my friends noticed I wasn't eating lunch at school. And then I'd have to explain what I was doing. My friends found it baffling.

All my life, people have usually reacted to my fasting in one of two ways: either they tell me it's dangerous and therefore foolhardy, or they tell me that it's just like missing lunch and therefore not a big deal. Neither of these is quite true: fasting in Islam is meant to be difficult but not dangerous. That's why fasting is not required for children, elderly people, pregnant women, those who are ill, menstruating women, those who are traveling, and nursing mothers. If someone becomes ill while fasting, then he is allowed to break his fast.

Fasting does make people hungry and thirsty and immensely tired. One of my friends calls it having "Ramadan brain," since it's so hard to think clearly. And even though being grumpy is a natural result of being hungry and thirsty and immensely tired, Muslims are supposed to transcend the grumpiness. Fasting doesn't just mean avoiding food and water—it means being extra patient and kind and refraining from fighting or arguing. I personally find it most challenging to be patient!

My friends who are not Muslim understand that fasting causes hunger and thirst. But they do not always realize that fasting also causes exhaustion. This is certainly because lack of liquids causes drowsiness and because our bodies lack the fuel required to feel energetic. But it's also because we have to drag ourselves out of bed for *suhoor*.

*Suhoor* is the Arabic name for the light predawn meal
that Muslims eat before the fast begins. Predawn? As in
around 4:00 a.m. or even earlier, while it is still pitch-dark?
Sadly for those of us who are not morning people, yes.

Since the fast begins at dawn, it is optional—though
recommended—to arise *before* dawn to eat a light meal.
Most Muslims arise for suhoor, eat their meal, wait a few
minutes until the arrival of dawn, pray the dawn prayer,
and then—if they're lucky—go back to sleep before getting up for work or school.

The prayer timetables in Chapter 3 also show the exact time that the fast begins, which is at the start of the
Fajr prayer time. The suhoor and all predawn eating must
end a few minutes *before* Fajr. As the tables show, the
starting time of Fajr can vary considerably, depending
upon the time of year and the geographical location. That
means that the time I set my alarm for suhoor can vary
considerably, too. It's a lot easier to fast in the winter than
in the summer, because the days are shorter.

It is not easy to get to sleep early enough to wake
brightly before dawn. And food looks unappetizing at
such an early hour. For those of us who attend school or
work in countries where most people do not fast, opportunities to rest throughout the day are scarce.

For suhoor, I usually eat an egg or peanut butter on
toast, but everyone has different preferences, and there
are no requirements about what can be eaten. I drink lots
of water. After finishing my predawn meal, I voice the
intention to fast. The intention to fast is required and

may be stated in any language. In English, it might be, "I intend to fast today for Ramadan."

Once the intention to fast has been undertaken, the fast cannot be broken until sunset. Breaking a fast on purpose is a sin. (In fact, a Muslim who breaks a fast intentionally may be required to fast sixty more consecutive days to atone for it!) However, there's an exception to this rule: a Muslim can break a fast intentionally if his health is endangered. In this case, the fast can be terminated and "made up" after Ramadan.

"Cheating a little" while fasting, like purposely eating or drinking a little bit, is not allowed, and it invalidates the fast. *Accidentally* eating or drinking does not invalidate the fast. A Muslim who accidentally breaks a fast must simply (and doggedly) resume fasting as if nothing had happened.

And accidents do happen. One year, when I was in eighth grade or so, my younger brother's birthday fell during Ramadan. He was too young to fast, but I was fasting amid all the cake and ice cream and lemonade.

"We'll save you some birthday cake for later," said my mother, who, though fasting herself, was apparently unmoved by cravings for chocolate-banana layer cake (my favorite). "Oh, and can you go make some more lemonade? They're pinning the tail on the donkey."

I retrieved the can of lemonade concentrate from the freezer, emptied the slushy, crystalline, lemony mass into a pitcher, and carefully measured out three cans of cold water to mix into it. As my wooden spoon chased the last spiraling yellow blob around the pitcher, I did what I always do: I raised a spoonful to my mouth to taste it.

When my mother bustled into the kitchen a few seconds later to check on my progress, she saw me standing frozen by the jug of swirling lemonade, the incriminating, lazily dripping spoon still clutched in my raised hand.

She smiled and said, "You didn't break your fast intentionally. Accidentally breaking a fast is a gift from God, because God made you forget. Bring the lemonade with you when you come out."

Later, my mother told me a story about being a teenager in a small town in India when Ramadan fell during the blazing hot season. Temperatures reached 120°F. Air-conditioning was only a distant dream.

While fasting one scorching day, my mother noticed, as if it had only just appeared, the pitcher of cold water that habitually sat on the wooden side table against the wall. She reached out, filled a glass, and drank it all in one thirsty movement. She closed her eyes in relief, and only then realized that she had broken her fast.

"Why didn't you tell me not to drink it?" she demanded in frustration of her older brother. He had been reading, sitting on a cushion across the room. He had silently watched the entire episode.

"You must have needed the water badly," he replied, closing the book. "When you accidentally break a fast, God has made you forget, because you need to, and it's not up to us to rebuke or interrupt you."

Fasting is required for healthy adults. Children

typically start fasting gradually, or with "training fasts." For example, they might attempt a half-day fast, or a fast in which they can drink but not eat. When I first started fasting myself, I fasted for only a day or two the first year, then for a few more days the second year, and so on, until I eventually fasted the whole month.

In Islam, fasting is not *required* until after puberty. But some Muslim parents allow their children to fast before puberty, if they desire. Children are often eager to try fasting, and their parents do not want to discourage them.

On the other hand, some Muslim parents believe that children should not fast before puberty, because they are still growing and developing. When Islam was born fourteen hundred years ago, children who had passed puberty were considered adults in all cultures. Therefore, these parents believe that fasting is required only for healthy adults.

This is why, if Ramadan falls during the school year, you may come across some Muslims in your classrooms who are fasting and some who are not. Those who are fasting might have trouble explaining why they are fasting or why they are tired. Those who are not fasting might have trouble explaining why they're *not* fasting when others are. In either case, they and their parents are making different personal religious choices.

Unexpected challenges may lurk behind classroom doors for those students who do fast during school hours. While fasting when I was in high school, I once arrived at my afternoon health class hungry and already tired from my morning classes. On this particular day, my teacher began the Nutrition Unit by showing us a movie about *food*.

There I was, fasting, my stomach grumbling embarrassingly, forced to watch a movie filled with all the food that was *not* nutritious (but beautifully tempting), like cookies, cakes, ice cream, candy, potato chips, and Cracker Jack. Thank goodness I couldn't smell it, too!

I still remember this episode as funny, but difficult, though it has been many years since it happened. It illustrates why fasting is meant to be difficult in Islam—it makes a greater impact than if it were an easy thing to do. What exactly, then, are Muslims supposed to learn from fasting?

The first reason Muslims fast is that the Qur'an tells us to fast, as did Muhammad. Indeed, fasting is one of the Five Pillars. Ramadan, the month of fasting, is the month in which the Prophet Muhammad received the first words of the Qur'an from the angel Gabriel; this makes Ramadan especially holy for Muslims.

Secondly, Ramadan requires Muslims to learn discipline and to challenge themselves. I heard a speaker at a local mosque say recently, "You're not fasting for God. God does not need your hunger and thirst. God tells you to fast for *yourself*, to test yourself. It is easy to be kind and generous when you are fed and comfortable. It is much harder when you are hungry and thirsty."

Therefore, fasting teaches *discipline*, which is valued in Islam. Discipline can help me carefully think through my decisions so I don't rush into them. Discipline can help me work hard at acquiring a skill, like practicing a musical instrument every day. And discipline can help me do something I ought to do, even if I would rather not—like washing dishes or taking out the trash.

A third reason for fasting is to experience just a little bit of what it must be like to starve. According to UNICEF, someone in the world dies of hunger-related causes about once every three and a half seconds. This sobering statistic can certainly cause us to feel compassion. But fasting adds to this compassion by making us feel it *physically* as well as emotionally.

The Ramadan fast is not truly like starving, because we can eat as much as we like after sunset, unlike those who do not ever get enough to eat. Even so, fasting does require us to feel physical discomfort. That physical discomfort is a constant reminder of hunger; it's a shadow of what it must be like to starve. In a way, fasting forces us to understand starvation with both our brains and our bodies; when we fast, we are constantly reminded that we cannot simply open the refrigerator and eat whenever we hear our stomachs rumble.

Finally, fasting helps us disregard our bodily needs for a while and concentrate on more spiritual things, such as reflecting on what is important in life, trying to improve ourselves, or thinking about how to improve our relationships with people. In addition, when Muslims fast, our hunger and thirst remind us continually that we are fasting because our religion tells us to fast, and that in turn helps us feel closer to God.

It is commonly accepted in many cultures that fasting can help connect people to God or religion. That is why so many religions include some form of fasting. Catholics fast on Ash Wednesday and Good Friday, and Jews fast on Yom Kippur. Hindus and Buddhists fast on certain days as well.

During the seventh century, when the Prophet Muhammad came upon Jews fasting on Yom Kippur, he told his own followers to fast with them, in solidarity. That's why I fast on Yom Kippur as well as during Ramadan. I also know that some Christians fast during Ramadan, in solidarity with Muslims. In 2001, Pope John Paul II urged Catholics to fast one day during Ramadan. So you might say that fasting sometimes connects people of different faiths to each other, as well as to God.

Although I have been relating the challenges of fasting, I must also mention that Muslims are proud of fasting. It is an achievement. Despite the difficulties, Muslims look forward to Ramadan. It is a time of celebration as well as reflection.

If I were not required to fast, I probably would never do it. But every year at Ramadan, I am grateful that I am required to fast, because it reminds me how fortunate I am. I sometimes think that it might be a good idea for every adult to try it, not for any religious reasons, but because I think fasting helps us feel empathy and compassion toward others.

Recently, I watched a television interview featuring Hamza and Husain Abdullah, two American Muslim professional football players who fast during their pre-season six-hour football practices. They do take precautions, drinking and eating as much as possible before dawn and ensuring that their coaches know if they feel faint or overheated. In the interview, Hamza Abdullah's head coach, Ken Whisenhunt of the Arizona Cardinals, expressed admiration for Hamza's commitment.[2]

Hamza and Husain Abdullah grew up watching Hakeem Olajuwon play professional basketball. Olajuwon led the Houston Rockets to two NBA championships and was later inducted into the Basketball Hall of Fame. He played the center position on the court, and many consider him one of the best centers to ever play basketball. A Muslim, Olajuwon fasted during his professional basketball games when they fell during Ramadan. Fasting did not seem to dim his performance; in 1995, Ramadan fell during February, the same month Olajuwon was named NBA Player of the Month. Olajuwon himself may have grown up watching another American Muslim basketball player, one of the all-time best: Kareem Abdul-Jabbar.

These athletes are unusual, though, and most people do not physically exert themselves during Ramadan. But once, when I was in high school, I found myself running a mile without water. It happened because I was too embarrassed and self-conscious to appear different from my classmates.

I had arrived at school, fasting, to learn that we were scheduled to run the mile for the Presidential Physical

Fitness Test that day. I didn't want to tell my teacher I
was fasting, because I was afraid he would think I was
making excuses. But neither did I want to run a mile in
the heat when I couldn't drink any water. I didn't know
what to do.

I finally chose to run and not tell anyone. In retro-
spect, I do not think this was a wise decision, as sunset
was many hours away. I cannot remember my time, but I
do consider my not collapsing in a fit of exhaustion to be
a moral victory!

## When Is Ramadan?

Because Ramadan is on the Islamic calendar, it shifts
from year to year. This means that, every year, Ramadan
arrives ten or eleven days earlier than it did the previous
year. Ramadan began on August 11 in 2010, but on August 1 in 2011.[3]

The reason it moves has to do with the nature of the
Islamic calendar, which is lunar, or based on the moon.
Lunar calendars were common in antiquity, probably because the moon's phases were clear and obvious to the
naked eye. It was easy to count the days from new moon
to new moon and understand that this process took
twenty-nine or thirty days.

The Islamic calendar comprises twelve lunar months,
all twenty-nine or thirty days long. "Ramadan" is the
name of the ninth month. The first day of each lunar
month begins the morning after the new moon appears.

Ramadan arrives ten or eleven days earlier every year because of the discrepancy between the lunar calendar and the *solar* calendar, the one based on the sun. Although Ramadan is on the lunar calendar, we in the modern world use the solar calendar. The lunar year is ten or eleven days shorter than the solar year.

What happens if your calendar is eleven days shorter than the one everyone else uses? Well, *your* New Year's Day arrives eleven days earlier than *their* New Year's Day, because your lunar year terminates and starts over again while they still have eleven more days to go. In fact, all the holidays on the Islamic lunar calendar arrive eleven days earlier that year, for the same reason.

Not all lunar calendars operate like the Islamic calendar. The Jewish calendar and the Hindu calendar are also lunar, but both of those are adjusted every few years so that the holidays remain in the same season. In other words, if the calendars become too unaligned with the solar calendar, then extra days are added to realign them. Because the Islamic calendar is not adjusted, Ramadan just keeps moving ten or eleven days earlier every year. In thirty-three years, it comes back to where it started.

In some ways, this is frustrating for Muslims, because Ramadan cannot be associated with seasonal traditions, the way Christmas in the Northern Hemisphere is associated with wintertime or Independence Day with summer barbecues. On the other hand, it does seem more *fair* to let Ramadan move through the year. This way, no one is stuck with long, hot fasts every single year while Muslims in the opposite hemisphere get short, cool fasts every year!

## Ramadan Traditions Around the World

Ramadan traditions differ according to country and culture. American Muslim cultural traditions for Ramadan are still evolving. But some Ramadan traditions are the same, no matter where in the world Muslims live.

It's traditional for all Muslims to invite family and friends for *iftar*, which is the dinner to break the fast at sunset. Many mosques in the United States now host public iftar dinners for community members, whatever their religion, at least once during Ramadan. In many countries, mosques offer free iftar dinners to those who cannot afford much to eat.

All Muslim cultures have traditional foods that are made during Ramadan, particularly sweets. It is customary to send food to neighbors, who sometimes send their own food in exchange. Muslims should also make extra efforts to feed the hungry during Ramadan.

Traditional foods eaten for iftar vary according to culture. But some foods are common throughout the world. If you should ever be invited to break the fast with Muslims, then almost certainly you will be offered a date. A date of the sticky, sweet, caramel-like fruit variety, of course.

The Prophet Muhammad had a custom of breaking his fast with dates, accompanied by milk or yogurt or water, so it is traditional for Muslims to do so. From the time I was small, I remember my mother drinking her glass of water at iftar, setting down the empty glass with a satisfied sigh, and murmuring, "Thanks to God; I feel alive again."

Although our family iftar usually consists of dates, lots of water, and fruit, I occasionally also make *lassi*, a sweet yogurt drink. Nearly all Muslim cultures around the world make some variety of yogurt drink: sweet, salty, carbonated, noncarbonated, mint-flavored, or rose-flavored. My favorite is a slightly sweet version flavored with pine essence, a flavor commonly used in India and Pakistan. In case you would like to try making lassi, here's an easy recipe:

**Lassi (Sweet Yogurt Drink)**

1 cup plain lowfat (my preference), nonfat, or
    whole milk yogurt
⅔ cup water
½ cup granulated sugar
2 tablespoons rose water* or ¼ teaspoon
    concentrated rose extract
Ice cubes

Whisk the yogurt until smooth. Add the water, sugar, and rose water. Whisk until the mixture is smooth and the sugar is dissolved. Pour over ice cubes and enjoy! Makes 4 servings.

*Rose water is available in many supermarkets, but if you can't find it, try an Indian, Middle Eastern, or Persian market. Use more than 2 tablespoons, if you like.

I nurture the goal of tasting every traditional Ramadan food in the world. I have not yet progressed significantly, but high on my list is *güllaç*. In Turkey, Muslims make güllaç for Ramadan evenings. A dessert resembling a custard, güllaç involves cooking special wafers in rose-scented cream sauce. According to Turkish tradition, güllaç is so tricky to make that the cook must recite prayers over the güllaç mixture or it will not attain the correct consistency!

Another dish that the Turks make during Ramadan has a fun story behind it. Sometimes, a Turkish religious leader will give his congregation triangular amulets with folded verses of the Qur'an inside. During Ramadan, Turks make a culinary version of this amulet, called *muska*. These are triangular deep-fried pastries with a sweet quince filling.

Several types of cookies have been checked off my list of Ramadan foods to try. Every year, my children invite their friends over to make holiday cards and Ramadan cookies. Our Ramadan cookies are inspired by—but not exactly equivalent to—the various types of traditional Ramadan cookies, such as *ghourayebeh, mamoul,* and *kahk,* found in Middle Eastern countries. Here's my recipe:

### Ramadan Cookies

If your supermarket does not carry these ingredients, try Middle Eastern, Persian, or Indian markets. Or try an online Middle Eastern grocery store.

*For the filling:*
1 cup finely chopped dates (I like Medjool dates)
    or 1 8-ounce package of date paste
½ cup shredded sweetened coconut

*For the cookies:*
1 cup (2 sticks) butter
1 cup powdered sugar
1 teaspoon vanilla (I use nonalcoholic vanilla
    extract or ground vanilla beans)
2 tablespoons rose water (optional)
2 tablespoons orange-flower water (optional)
1 egg
2¼ cups all-purpose flour

*For decoration:*
½ cup powdered sugar for dusting

Preheat the oven to 325° F. Mix the dates and the coconut together in a bowl and set aside. If you're using date paste, break or chop it into pea-sized pieces and mix it with the coconut.

With an electric mixer or food processor, mix the butter and ½ cup powdered sugar until creamy. Add the vanilla, rose water, orange-flower water, and egg, and mix until just blended. Stir in the flour *gently* with a wooden spoon, and stop as soon as the flour is mixed into the batter.

Handle the dough lightly, and try not to rub it or roll it too much, or the butter will start to separate and the cookies will become tough.

If the dough is too soft or oily, refrigerate it for 30 minutes. Otherwise, take a lump of dough, roll it into a 1½-inch ball, and make a depression in the ball with your thumb. Put ½ teaspoon or so of the date mixture into the depression and close the dough around it to seal it. Put the ball on a cookie sheet and flatten it slightly. Make all the cookies this way.

Bake until the cookies are just beginning to turn light golden in color, about 30 minutes. Let them cool on the cookie sheet. Sift powdered sugar over the cookies or roll them in powdered sugar. Makes about 2 dozen cookies.

Egypt has some of the most colorful Ramadan traditions. In Egypt, artisans craft Ramadan lanterns from recycled materials like broken glass bottles and old tin cans. Shop awnings lining the streets in Cairo bow under the glittering weight of hundreds of multicolored, multifaceted Ramadan lanterns for sale. They range in size from small hand-held lanterns the size of handbags to lanterns standing several feet high. When candles are placed inside, the colored-glass surfaces sparkle like jewels.

After Egyptians break their fasts at sunset, streets all over the city come alive with people buying food or visiting friends. That is when groups of children traditionally take their Ramadan lanterns in hand, light the candles within, and walk down the streets, chanting an Egyptian song thousands of years old—so ancient that some parts of it have no known meaning anymore. As the children sing, adults give them fruits or nuts or sweets. It seems a bit like caroling at Christmas or even trick-or-treating at Halloween. This is the song they sing:

> *Wahawi, ya wahawi,*
> *Iyyaha,*
> *You have gone, O Sha'ban,*
> *You have come, O Ramadan,*
> *Iyyahah,*
> *The daughter of the Sultan*
> *Is wearing her caftan,*
> *Iyyahah,*
> *For God the Forgiver,*
> *Give us this season's gift.*[4]

In the song, "Sha'ban" refers to the month before Ramadan. The "daughter of the Sultan" wears her caftan because she's preparing to go to the mosque. And "this season's gift" may refer to the gifts that children receive at the end of Ramadan, for Eid al-Fitr (described in the next chapter).⁵

In India, my mother used to make paper lanterns during Ramadan. When my kids were small, we used to make our own Ramadan lanterns with glass jars that we covered with translucent tissue paper of many colors. We dropped tea candles inside and lit them at sunset.

## The Night of Power

The last ten days of Ramadan are especially holy to Muslims. The anniversary of *Laylat al-Qadr*, or "the Night of Power," falls during those last ten days. The Night of Power is the anniversary of the night that the Prophet Muhammad first received the words of God, according to Muslim tradition. It is the anniversary of the date that the first words of the Qur'an were revealed. (This is described further in Chapter 11.)

But which of the last ten days is it, exactly? Nobody knows.

The most likely date for the Night of Power, Muslims believe, is the twenty-seventh night of Ramadan. This belief is based on certain sayings attributed to the Prophet Muhammad. On the Night of Power, prayer assumes greater importance than usual, and Muslims believe their prayers are more likely to be fulfilled than at other times of the year. Some Muslims stay up all night praying, taking breaks to socialize and eat, and then praying some more. Since no one is sure exactly which night is the

Night of Power, some people play it safe by praying extra hard during all ten nights.

Ramadan is a month of hunger and thirst and fatigue for Muslims, but it's also a festive time. It means many things to us: discipline, compassion, piety, festivity, connecting with other Muslims, connecting with people of other religions, connecting with God, extra appreciation of food and drink, extra consciousness of good deeds and charity, and a sense of achievement.

## Chapter 5

## Holidays: From Turkey Dinner to Baklava

With its glittering decorations festooning everything from houses to streetlights, Christmas was beautiful, even to me as a Muslim kid growing up in California. And it was everywhere, for months, resulting in vacation from school, Santa Clauses, lots of presents, pretty music wafting through department stores, fruitcake and cookies, and pageants and parades. The two Muslim holidays, unheard of by my acquaintances and celebrated by only a small religious minority, just couldn't compete.

My parents tried their best, but it is not easy to produce an atmosphere of festivity and celebration when you know hardly anyone who celebrates the holiday and it doesn't even appear on calendars. No Eid decorations appear in department stores (or anywhere else), and there's no months-long buildup of tinsel, lights, music, traditional food, school holiday projects, holiday television specials, and holiday movies. Of course, my Hindu and Jewish friends faced the same holiday challenges. For all of us, the inevitable questions about what we got for Christmas were awkward.

Some Muslims do participate in Christmas celebrations, just as some Jews do. Some may enjoy the non-religious aspects of Christmas and enjoy participating for that reason alone. Others may participate because they have Christian family members. My husband's mother is Christian, so we help her celebrate Christmas.

But when I was growing up, Christmas wasn't my holiday. And I was always guiltily disappointed in Eid. That's why my absolutely favorite holiday was Thanksgiving.

I *loved* Thanksgiving. I loved making turkey-shaped place cards, and I loved pumpkin pie. I loved turkey and gravy and mashed potatoes and candied yams and stuffing and cranberry sauce (even though jamlike stuff and meat is a combination alien to the Indian-Pakistani palate). One of my father's colleagues invited us to his house every year for Thanksgiving dinner. His wife made everything from scratch, from fluffy white dinner rolls to thick, steaming gravy.

Now I make the entire traditional Thanksgiving dinner myself. I love celebrating a holiday that everyone else in the country is celebrating. I can celebrate as a Muslim and as an American, because everyone understands giving thanks.

## Eid al-Fitr

The next best holiday for me, after Thanksgiving, was Eid. *Eid* simply means "festival," and Muslims celebrate two *eid*s. Because "Eid" is a phonetic spelling of an Arabic word, you might see the word spelled *Id* or *'Id* or *Aid*. It is an English-language approximation.

*Eid al-Fitr* means "Festival of the Fast-Breaking," and it is held the day after Ramadan ends, on the first day of the next lunar month, Shawwal. Eid al-Fitr (or just "Eid") is the Arabic name for this festival, but the name varies according to country. In Turkey, Eid al-Fitr is called *Şeker Bayrami*, or "Sugar Festival." In Malaysia, it is called *Hari Raya Puasa*, and in Indonesia it is called *Lebaran*. Sometimes it's called the "Little Eid."

On Eid al-Fitr, Muslims celebrate the accomplishment of fasting for Ramadan, and we give thanks for our blessings. Food is a central part of the celebration.

Muslims throughout the world celebrate Eid in different ways, but some traditions are common to all. Special Eid prayers are held at mosques in the mornings. Muslims give extra charity on Eid, if they can afford to. It is also common, in most countries, to wear clothes that are special or new, or both.

Some people get very dressed up to go to Eid prayers and some do not. In India and Pakistan, Eid is a formal occasion. In my family, an Indian American one, dressing up was serious business. For us, Eid was nearly as formal as an Indian-Pakistani wedding, to which guests always wore their very best finery. Under the new Eid clothes, though, it is also traditional to wear at least one item of clothing that is old or torn. This reminds us to stay humble and not peacock too much in our new feathers.

My mother often stayed up late the night before Eid, sewing shimmering, silky Indian outfits for me; sometimes these were embroidered or sparkling with brocade. Boys often wore black vests with gold embroidery, worn over white shirts; sometimes they wore *shirvanis* (long fitted coats worn over tight trousers). My mother usually wore a sari, and my father wore a suit. These days, sometimes I wear American clothes to the mosque on Eid, and sometimes I wear Indian clothes.

After prayers, Muslims visit friends and family, and adults give gifts to children. In India and Pakistan, gifts of money are common, but my parents often gave chocolates. I like to give gift-wrapped presents. One of my personal American Muslim traditions is to concoct an Eid-present treasure hunt for my kids.

A common Eid tradition all over the world is to ask forgiveness of family and acquaintances. In most Muslim cultures, the elderly are particularly respected, and various traditions reflect this attitude. For example, in Malaysia, children kneel before elders and kiss their hands, requesting a blessing. In Turkey, it is traditional for a child to kiss an elder person's hand and raise it to her forehead; the elder's response is to kiss the child on both cheeks.

In the Indian-Pakistani community, women paint henna patterns on their hands the night before Eid. *Chand Raat,* or "Night of the Moon," is the night the new moon is sighted, signaling that the next day is Eid. Stores remain open late and some offer henna painting. Muslims shop for last-minute Eid necessities, and in some cultures, children receive their new clothes on Chand Raat rather than the next day, on Eid.

For many years, we invited all our friends, regardless of religious background, to celebrate Eid with us. We sprinkled rose water on them when they arrived, to welcome them to our house. We also offered them—whether they were men, women, or children—a bit of scent for their wrists, a tradition from India. We served dinner for sixty people and gave gifts to all the children. I painted their hands with henna. Upon departing, guests received small pouches of dates and candied almonds for good luck.

Traditional Eid al-Fitr food depends upon the country and culture. In India and Pakistan, Muslims make *sheer khurma,* a creamy milk pudding filled with thread-thin noodles, raisins, pistachios, saffron, and pine essence. In my family, we eat sheer khurma for Eid breakfast, after Eid prayers, and then we eat it at any house we may happen to visit on Eid. Almost every Indian or Pakistani Muslim family makes sheer khurma, and traditionally it is rude to not taste it wherever you go, even if you have been eating sheer khurma all day and cannot face another bite.

In Egypt, *kahk* is most commonly associated with Eid. "Kahk" is the name for round white cookies filled with dates or nuts and dusted with icing sugar. In Jordan, Eid dessert might be *konefeh al-id,* a syrup-soaked dessert made from layers of shredded pastry filled with white cheese. In Turkey, Muslims might prepare *lokma,* fried doughnutlike balls soaked in syrup, or *zerde,* sweet, syrupy saffron-and-fruit rice. Palestinians might make *qatayef,* which are honey pancakes filled with sweet cheese or nuts. In Indonesia, sticky rice cakes called *ketupat* are cooked in leaves from the coconut palm tree.

In Malaysia, *ice kacang* might be served for Eid dessert. Imagine a bowl containing a mixture of red beans, chopped fruit, fine noodles, and little fruit-flavored jellied cubes. Now top this whole multicolored mixture with a mound of shaved ice. Finally, pour some flavored syrups (you choose the combination) and coconut milk over the whole thing. Your ice kacang is now ready to eat!

Celebrating Eid in North America means a variety of foods, because Muslims here come from diverse ethnic backgrounds. In the United States, the three largest groups of American Muslims are South Asians (Indian, Pakistani, Sri Lankan, and Afghan), Middle Easterners, and African Americans whose families have been in the United States for centuries. At an Eid potluck in America, you might find dishes from all these cultural traditions.

South Asians might bring sheer khurma or *biriyani,* a dish of spiced rice and meat. Middle Easterners might bring grilled meat kebabs. Southeast Asians might bring ketupat with *rendang,* a beef dish. Moroccans might bring their famous national dish, *bastilla,* which is a chicken-and-egg pie cooked in a large, crispy pastry crust, all topped with almonds, powdered sugar, and cinnamon.

African American Muslims might bring Eid dinner dishes that resemble Thanksgiving dishes. An Eid brunch in the African American Muslim community might feature fried chicken, pancakes, salmon patties, homemade biscuits, eggs, and grits. And there might be bean pie for dessert.

If there is one food that is truly an original American Muslim food, it is bean pie. Although its origins are uncertain, bean pie was probably created in the 1930s, in New York City, in the community of African Americans who belonged to the "Nation of Islam." The Nation of Islam, despite its name, did not "break off" from Islam. It began separately from Islam in the early twentieth century, as a movement of African Americans trying to form their own identity. The members of the Nation of Islam were sometimes called Black Muslims. (The Nation of Islam is discussed further in Chapter 15.)

It was Black Muslims who invented bean pie. According to some accounts, Nation of Islam members invented it as part of their efforts to decrease their meat consumption and eat more beans. Concocting a dessert from beans was a new and slightly repulsive idea for many Americans (though it would not be so for Asians, who use beans in their desserts). One of the early bakers of the bean pie named it the South Park Special, because he was afraid nobody would eat it if he called it "bean pie"![1]

By 1980, most Black Muslims had converted to Sunni Islam. Black Muslims became Muslims. And bean pie was transformed from a Black Muslim food to a Muslim food. Today, bean pie is an original, uniquely African American Muslim food and is often featured at Eid celebrations.

I had never heard of bean pie before I wrote this book, but I tried making one, and it was delicious. I'm including my recipe here. You might want to experiment with it by adding fresh blueberries or mashed bananas or sweetened shredded coconut.

### African American Muslim Bean Pie

1 can navy beans
2 tablespoons butter
2 eggs
1 14-ounce can sweetened condensed milk
½ cup dark brown sugar
½ teaspoon ground nutmeg
1 teaspoon ground cinnamon
½ teaspoon salt
½ teaspoon ground ginger
½ teaspoon ground cloves

2 tablespoons vanilla extract (I use nonalcoholic
    vanilla or ground vanilla beans)
1 unbaked 9" piecrust

Preheat the oven to 425° F.

Combine everything except the piecrust in a
blender or food processor and puree. Pour into the
piecrust. Bake for 15 minutes.

Reduce heat to 350° F, and bake for another 35
minutes or until set.

Serve warm, plain or with whipped cream or ice
cream.

I love food traditions. I love how good-luck charms
are baked into English Christmas pudding and how Jewish honey cake symbolizes wishes for a sweet new year. I
love how, in Bulgaria, paper "fortunes" are baked into bread.
In the United States, perhaps more than any other country,
it's easy to find an exciting array of cultural traditions.

My mother-in-law recently sent me an interesting example of how ethnic traditions come to the United States.
She is originally from Sri Lanka, and she sent me a recipe
for *watalappan*. This is a caramel-coconut pudding that
has been passed down through the generations by Muslim
Sri Lankans whose ancestors came from Malaysia. And
now it has migrated to Eid tables in the United States.

In many countries, non-Muslims participate in Muslim
celebrations and vice versa. Christians in Lebanon participate in Eid celebrations and Lebanese Muslims

participate in Christmas celebrations. This is true in many parts of Asia and Africa, as well. And it's true in the United States.

## Eid al-Adha

Imagine a scene thousands of years ago, in a one-room house in the desert. A boy lies on his back on a rough bench, gazing trustingly up at his father, who stands beside him. A long, pointed knife gleams in the father's hand. Anguish is written on his face.

"Go ahead, Father," says the boy. "If God told you to sacrifice me, then you must."

The father bends down to cut the throat of his son, his heart dying within him. Then a miracle occurs. Just as the knife touches the boy's neck, God replaces the boy with a lamb. The lamb dies, and the boy is safe.

My Jewish friends recognize this story as one they know from their own religion. It appears in both the Old Testament and the Qur'an. The main difference is that, in the Muslim tradition, the boy to be sacrificed is Ismail, whereas in the Jewish and Christian traditions, it's his brother, Isaac. Despite the differences, the fact that all three monotheistic religions incorporate this story shows their common roots.

When I was young, I thought this a very strange tale. How could Abraham know exactly what God wanted? What if Abraham misinterpreted God's intent? Why would God tell someone to sacrifice his child?

For Muslims, this story teaches that human sacrifice is

not something God needs. Certain ancient cultures, like the Aztecs, did practice human sacrifice. The Abraham story advocates a *turning away* from this practice. It tells us that human sacrifice is not a necessary or desirable part of worship.

This story also illustrates the importance of obedience and commitment to God. Some religious stories are considered *parables,* which are stories designed to teach something or to illustrate a moral. Aesop's fables, for example, are parables. The story of the tortoise and the hare illustrates the moral "Slow and steady wins the race." Abraham's story of the sacrifice can be considered a parable, too.

Abraham's story is the basis for the second major Islamic festival, which arrives a few months after Ramadan. *Eid al-Adha,* or "Festival of the Sacrifice," commemorates Abraham's actions and God's mercy. It is sometimes called *Eid al-Kabir,* or "the Greater Eid." In Turkey it is called *Kurban Bayrami,* and in Malaysia it is called *Hari Raya Haji.*

It is traditional in all Muslim cultures to commemorate Abraham's actions by slaughtering an animal and donating the meat to the needy. A thousand or more years ago, donating fresh meat was a common method of giving charity. By incorporating food distribution into the Eid holiday, Muslims not only commemorated Abraham's sacrifice, but also gave themselves an extra occasion for charity.

Sometimes I see this slaughter of an animal on Eid al-Adha referred to as an "animal sacrifice." This is not a correct description. The slaughter of an animal for

Eid was never meant to be a "sacrifice" in the way, for example, Aztecs or Greeks or other ancient peoples undertook sacrifices to appease their god or gods. The Eid slaughter of an animal is not meant to appease God or atone for any sins. It is simply the humane (according to halal standards) slaughter of an animal whose meat is to be donated to the hungry (although it is allowable to keep a small portion of the meat for oneself). It is a method of giving charity that also commemorates Abraham's commitment to God.

In today's world, it might not be convenient or practical to slaughter an animal yourself and locate a poor person who needs raw meat, all before the meat spoils. (It's easier in a Muslim-majority country, where everyone understands this tradition.) That's why, today, many Muslims opt to give money to organizations that manage the slaughtering and donating for them. Or they just make a charitable donation of money.

Slaughtering an animal for Eid al-Adha is not required, but only recommended. Because Eid originated in a time and place where meat was a necessary part of the diet, it was only logical that charity took the form of donating meat. However, the real point of the holiday is to give charity and commemorate Abraham's absolute devotion to God. A gift of money to those who need it counts as charity, too.

In my family, because of vegetarian and spiritual considerations, we either donate money or donate a living animal rather than slaughter one. We buy an animal (like

a goat or some chickens) through a particular charitable
organization, and donate it to a needy family. Instead of a
one-time meal of meat, the family gets an ongoing food
source. The family can start a family farm and use the
animal for milk or eggs. This is not a traditional form of
Eid al-Adha charity, but we hope that it satisfies the spirit
of giving and celebration.

Hundreds of years ago, in the days before refrigeration, meat slaughtered on the day of Eid al-Adha
needed to be cooked that same day. That's why meat is
still the traditional Eid al-Adha holiday food. But Eid
al-Adha dishes vary according to geographical area and
culture. One of the most interesting, I think, is the Moroccan dish, *mrouzia*, a sweet and spicy concoction of
lamb, honey, raisins, almonds, and other spices.

Most of the other Eid al-Adha rituals are similar to
Eid al-Fitr rituals. Muslims attend the Eid prayer in the
morning. On this Eid, also, Muslims wear new clothes if
they can and give gifts to the children. They visit their
friends and families, and it is a time of both forgiving
people and asking for their forgiveness.

In Muslim-majority countries, Eid al-Adha is a public
holiday, often the biggest one of the year. In Turkey, a
five-day holiday is typical. In Singapore, Eid al-Adha is
called *Hari Raya Haji* and is a four-day festival.

## Miraj

In my family, we never celebrated the anniversary
of the Prophet's Night Journey and ascension to heaven,

which is described in Chapter 3. But in some Muslim communities, people decorate their homes with lights on this day, the twenty-seventh day of the Islamic month of Rajab. They also make a special trip to the mosque and gather children around them, over tea and sweets, to recite the story of the Prophet's Night Journey.

## Ashura

According to Muslim tradition, the day of *Ashura,* the tenth day of the Islamic month of Muharram, was originally a joyous day, because many happy events occurred on it, such as the landing of Noah's Ark. After 680 CE,[2] though, Ashura became the anniversary of a tragic event—the brutal death of the Prophet Muhammad's grandson.

Muhammad had only one surviving child, a daughter named Fatima. She grew up and married Ali, and their two sons were named Hasan and Husayn. (These are very popular names for Muslim boys, to this day.) Ashura marks the death of the younger son, Husayn, who was tragically killed in battle in the year 680.

Although the killing of the Prophet's grandson is a sorrowful event for *all* Muslims, the anniversary of this event, at Ashura, is observed almost entirely by the Shi'a. Shi'i Muslims make up 10 to 15 percent of the total Muslim population. Sunni Muslims make up 85 to 90 percent. (Sunni and Shi'a are discussed further in Chapter 15.)

Because Ashura is the anniversary of a tragedy, the rituals are sad, too. Ashura rituals involve mourning Husayn, preserving the memory of his death, and contemplating the evils of injustice and tyranny, against which Husayn was fighting. Shi'i communities commemorate the events surrounding Husayn's battle with parades, floats, plays, and storytellers. Processions and parades feature replicas of Husayn's tomb and are accompanied by mournful music.

In order to feel deep sorrow and grief, some (but not all) Shi'a beat their chests in mourning. Some go further and beat their own backs with sticks or chains. A minority cut themselves with swords or knives. The goal of those who practice this *self-flagellation* is not to inflict serious damage, which is prohibited by Islam. Their purpose is to experience deep sadness for Husayn's death. Most Shi'a do not practice this self-flagellation.

Sunni Muslims condemn self-flagellation, and some Shi'i Muslims do as well. Some Shi'i religious leaders have recommended that those commemorating Ashura donate blood to hospital blood banks instead of self-flagellation. In Afghanistan, thousands of Shi'a have donated blood to hospitals on Ashura.[3]

The concept of suffering physical pain in a religious context occurs in other religions as well as in Shi'i Islam. In the Christian tradition, for example, beating oneself with a stick or whip has been a known practice for centuries, especially as a penance or as a way of becoming closer to God. Hinduism, too, has a tradition of inflicting pain on the self, such as through walking on red-hot coals.

In a few countries, non-Shi'a participate in Ashura,

too. In India, a small number of Sunni Muslims and even some Hindus participate in Ashura rituals. In Trinidad, Ashura is called *Hosay* and is celebrated by just about everyone, Muslim and non-Muslim alike. Hosay lasts for three nights and a day and is marked by colorful parades.

## Milad an-Nabi

This holiday celebrates the birthday of the Prophet Muhammad. I never realized it was a holiday when I was growing up. Perhaps it was hard enough for our small Muslim community to even celebrate the two Eids. But, in recent years in the United States, the Prophet's birthday has been celebrated with increasing frequency.

It falls on the twelfth day of the month of Rabi' al-Awwal and may be celebrated with special sermons at the mosques, retellings of the Prophet's life, holiday food, and live traditional religious music. (An infinitesimal minority of Muslims consider music to be un-Islamic, but the overwhelmingly vast majority of Muslims enjoy all kinds of music.) I recently attended a Milad an-Nabi celebration in which five musicians played traditional religious Moroccan music and the whole Muslim congregation clapped and danced and sang along.

The table on the next page lists all the months of the Islamic lunar calendar, with the holidays listed on the right. The names of the months are associated with the solar seasons. Because the names are ancient, they have a number of possible meanings and spellings.

# The Islamic Calendar

| MONTH NUMBER AND NAME | MEANING OF THE NAME | HOLIDAYS IN THIS MONTH |
|---|---|---|
| 1 Muharram | The sacred month | The New Year, Ashura |
| 2 Safar | The "vacant month" or "month of whistling of wind" | |
| 3 Rabi' al-Awwal | The first spring | Milad an-Nabi (Prophet's birthday) |
| 4 Rabi' al-Thani | The second spring | |
| 5 Jumada al-Awwal | The first month of dryness | |
| 6 Jumada al-Thani | The second month of dryness | |
| 7 Rajab | The revered month | Miraj (Ascension and Night Journey) |
| 8 Sha'ban | The month of division | |
| 9 Ramadan | The month of great heat | Fasting; Laylat al-Qadr (the Night of Power) |
| 10 Shawwal | The month of hunting | Eid al-Fitr (Festival of the Fast Breaking) |
| 11 Dhu al-Qa'da | The month of rest | |
| 12 Dhu al-Hijja | The month of pilgrimage | Hajj; Eid al-Adha (Festival of the Sacrifice) |

Chapter 6

## Donating to Charity

Muslims are expected to give extra charity during holidays and Ramadan, but also whenever they can. Charity is an ongoing obligation in Islam. In Arabic, this donation to charity is called *zakat*. It's one of the Five Pillars of Islam.

The following story illustrates the importance of charity in Islam:[1]

Imagine the desert of the Arabian peninsula nearly fourteen hundred years ago. Sand drifts everywhere, into the hunched one-room houses, onto the floors, into the food. Summer temperatures routinely reach 115° F. Rain dampens the desert floor only a few times a year, and when it neglects to fall, the crops die, the food stores diminish, and the danger of starvation occupies every-one's mind.

In the year 640, eight years after the death of the Prophet Muhammad, rain has proved fickle. Local food sources are scarce. The desert dwellers begin to hope for visits from merchant caravans, long parades of camels and wagons that bring food and other items for sale.

One day, a rider gallops into town to report the approach of a huge caravan of a thousand camels. The caravan belongs to Uthman ibn Affan, a wealthy merchant and one of the Prophet's companions and followers. The merchants of the town rush to the caravan, hoping to buy Uthman's wares to resell to the people of the town.

The merchants surround the lead wagons like ants around a honey cake, offering Uthman price after price for his food. Because food is scarce in this drought-stricken month, the merchants know that Uthman can charge any price he wishes, and the townspeople, desperate, will pay whatever they can.

But Uthman refuses to sell at any price.

"Oh, no," he says cheerfully, "I already have a better offer."

The merchants band together and offer him more money for the food. But Uthman smiles and refuses.

"I have a better offer," he repeats.

After futile pleading, the exasperated merchants finally demand just who it is who has offered so much more to Uthman.

"It is God, you see," replies Uthman. "God has offered

me many times the value of my goods if I give them away in charity. God says to 'give in charity what is good of what you have earned ... do not choose to give what is bad as alms'" (2:267).

Uthman reminds the merchants of what the Qur'an says: that if we give one grain of corn in charity, then God will grant us seven ears of corn in return, with a *hundred* grains of corn on each ear (2:261). According to Uthman, this is a much better offer than that of the merchants.

So Uthman unloads his caravan of food in the market-place the next day and his servant calls the townspeople: "Come to the square! This food is free for anyone in need! It is a gift from God!"

Four years later, Uthman becomes the *caliph*, the po-litical leader of the Muslim community.

Muslims must donate a set percentage of their total wealth to charity. This percentage varies between 2.5 and 20 percent, depending on the sect. This donation, zakat, is a religious obligation. Muslims are also urged to donate above the zakat amount, according to what they can afford. The Qur'an urges charity repeatedly, in over fifty verses. The Qur'an gives some examples of those who should receive charity, including the poor and needy, or-phans, relatives, travelers, and those who owe a crippling amount of money.

The following story comes from Muslim tradition:

Abraham, the prophet, always offered passing travel-ers some food and a place to stay for the night. One day, the story goes, an old man passed Abraham's house.

Abraham invited him inside and offered him dinner and a bed. The man accepted. As they sat down to eat, Abraham thanked God for his meal. Yet he noticed that the old man said nothing before he began to eat.

"Wait!" cried Abraham. "Do you not thank God before starting to eat the food He has given you?"

"I am not of your faith," said the old man. "I worship fire."

Abraham was so annoyed by this that he expelled the old man from his house. But as the old man wandered away, the angel Gabriel appeared to Abraham.

"God has been feeding this old man for seventy years, Abraham," said the angel reprovingly. "Yet you turn him out because you cannot tolerate him for one meal?"

Ashamed, Abraham dashed out the door after the old man. Apologizing for his behavior, he brought him back home to finish his dinner and spend the night.

This story clearly illustrates that a person's religion does not bar Muslims from offering the person charity or kindness. Charity can be given to anyone, whether the person is Muslim or not. Charity and kindness are intertwined concepts. An Islamic saying tells us that a smile is a charity. Removing an obstacle from the road is a charity, too.

Charity is one of the basic principles not only of Islam but of most other religions as well. It is also a universal value. A person need not belong to any religion to be charitable, but sometimes religion makes people more charitable than they would otherwise be.

## Chapter 7

# A Muslim Pilgrim's Progress

A pilgrimage is a visit to a sacred or special place, undertaken to pay respects. Often, it involves a long journey. Pilgrimage is a concept common to many religions.

In Islam, the most important pilgrimage is the *Hajj*, the pilgrimage to the city of Mecca in what is now Saudi Arabia. For Muslims, Mecca is holy because it is the birthplace of the Prophet Muhammad and home to the Ka'ba. Every Muslim who can afford it must perform the Hajj once in a lifetime. The Hajj is one of the Five Pillars of Islam.

The Hajj deeply affects those who participate in it. Muslims report feeling closer to God on the Hajj. They

also feel a deep emotional tie to the other millions of
Muslims who are there with them, chanting the same
prayers and worshiping together. Being part of such a
vast group gives Muslims a profound sense of being part
of a worldwide community.

The Hajj takes place during the Islamic month of
Dhu al-Hijja, beginning on the eighth day and ending on
the twelfth day. Eid al-Adha falls during the Hajj, on the
tenth day of Dhu al-Hijja.

The Hajj begins at the Ka'ba, an ancient cubical building of uncertain age. Muslims believe that Abraham and
his son, Ismail, built the Ka'ba. The Muslim story of the
Ka'ba goes like this:

When Adam, the first man God created, was expelled
from heaven, God gave him a sacred black stone. The
stone was eventually given to Abraham and Ismail. When
they built the Ka'ba for the worship of God, they embedded the Black Stone in it. By the time Muhammad was
born, centuries after Abraham and Ismail built the Ka'ba,
the original purpose of the Ka'ba had been forgotten.
The building had been filled with idols, which were stat-
ues representing the deities of the local pagan religion
(a polytheistic religion). It was no longer a shrine to one
God. When Muhammad eventually returned to Mecca
from Medina, where he and his followers had taken
refuge, he destroyed the idols and rededicated the Ka'ba
to God.

This is the story of the Ka'ba from Muslim tradition.
For Muslims, therefore, the Ka'ba represents nearly the

whole of Islamic sacred history, because its story begins with Adam, continues with Abraham, and achieves completion with Muhammad.

Every year, over two and a half million Muslims perform the Hajj. The number of pilgrims during the Hajj equals more than three times the entire population of the city of San Francisco.[1] Managing crowds this size is not easy, especially if you consider the complicating fact that the pilgrims speak many different languages and come from various cultures. That makes communicating even more of a challenge, particularly in an emergency.

That is why the Saudi government limits the number of Muslims who can attend the Hajj every year—many Muslims are turned away. It's a matter of safety and capacity. Even the "limited" number is so huge that people get jostled and pushed and sometimes injured. Pilgrims have even been trampled to death because of the sheer number of people.

During the week or two around Hajj, it therefore makes sense to allow only Muslims to enter Mecca and Medina, as the crowds are dangerously huge. And, because the Hajj is a religious duty for Muslims, but not a religious duty for non-Muslims, it is fair to give Muslims priority.

But what about non-Muslims visiting Mecca and Medina at times when the Hajj is not taking place? The Saudis prohibit non-Muslims from visiting Mecca and Medina at any time.

This is not a religious prohibition. *Islam* does

not prohibit non-Muslims from entering Mecca and
Medina. The Prophet himself never barred non-Muslims
from visiting Mecca and Medina. In fact, Muslim tradition relates an occasion on which the Prophet Muhammad allowed visiting Christians to use his own mosque
for their Christian prayers.

The reason for prohibiting non-Muslims from visiting Mecca and Medina may arise from practical considerations regarding *Umrah*, which is a shortened version
of the Hajj performed at a non-Hajj time. It is a kind of
"lesser pilgrimage" in Islam. Millions of Muslims perform Umrah every year, at any time except during Hajj.
Therefore, in order to keep the crowds down, while
allowing as many Muslims to perform Umrah as possible,
it does make practical sense (though it seems unfair) to
exclude the people who do not need to be there for their
religion and are coming only for tourism.

Tourism can create conflicts with religious duties.
Going to Mecca for Hajj or Umrah would cost me con-
siderable time and money, and I might be able to manage
it only once in my entire lifetime. It would be very frustrating if I finally got there only to find that my efforts to
perform the rituals and become closer to God were dis-
rupted by tourists. On the other hand, I think it is a
shame to permanently close off Mecca and Medina to
non-Muslims. Perhaps one day a compromise can be
reached.

One of the goals of the Hajj is to strive toward spiritual purity. In Islam, spiritual purity means unselfishness,

patience, compassion, and closeness to God. Muslims undertake certain actions in the hope of achieving it.

First, they leave behind any signs of wealth and status. Muslims may not wear jewelry or perfume on the Hajj, and they don plain clothing to emphasize their equality. Men wear garments made of two pieces of plain white cloth. Women wear any modest long-sleeved, floor-length clothing. They cover their hair while performing the Hajj, but covering faces is prohibited.

In his very last sermon, Muhammad made the following statement about equality:

> All mankind is from Adam and Eve. An Arab has no superiority over a non-Arab, and a non-Arab has no superiority over an Arab. A white person has no superiority over a black person, and a black person has no superiority over a white person. The most noble among you are those who are pious and engage in good actions.

Muslims reason that if everyone is equal in the eyes of God, except with respect to the good actions they perform, then everyone should *look* equal in the eyes of God, too, at least on the Hajj. That's why the pilgrims leave their jewelry and fancy clothes behind.

Spiritual purity also means being on your best behavior during the Hajj. Muslims are supposed to focus on their spiritual selves and avoid negative emotions like anger or impatience. Muslims must also refrain from killing any animals, even for food (except on Eid al-Adha), and from sexual relations. God should be the focus of all thoughts.

During the Hajj, Muslims perform traditional rituals in a particular order and on particular days. Several of these commemorate the story of Abraham, the same person who preached belief in one God and almost sacrificed his son to God. The Hajj is not so baffling when you understand Abraham's story. You may know the Old Testament story of Abraham. Here's the Islamic version of Abraham's story:

Abraham, called Ibrahim in Arabic, lived about four thousand years ago. Abraham had a son named Ismail. When Ismail was a baby, God told Abraham to take the baby and the baby's mother, Hajar, to the desert and leave them there. So he did.

I never understood this when I was young. Why would God order such a thing? Abraham's story is peppered with examples of his unconditional trust in God. The moral of his story is that it is important to trust God.

Following God's command, Abraham delivered Hajar and Ismail to the desert. Without food. Without water. Then he left.

When the baby began to cry, Hajar began searching for food and water. Becoming increasingly desperate, she began to run between the two nearby hills of Safa and Marwa, searching for water or for someone to help her.

The baby continued to cry, beating his heels upon the

ground and waving his tiny fists in the air. Just as Hajar began to lose hope, she witnessed something amazing. An angel materialized next to the screaming baby. The angel bent over the baby and pressed the baby's heel into the ground. Where Ismail's heel struck the sand, a stream of water spurted upward from the ground. It grew in strength until a stream flowed from Ismail down past Hajar's feet. The angel faded away and Hajar and her baby were saved.

In some versions of this story, the angel does not appear. Instead, God simply causes a spring to erupt where the baby's heel strikes the ground. In either case, Muslims believe that God protected Hajar and Ismail and caused the miracle of water to spring up under the baby's heel.

Hajar and Ismail settled there, near the stream, and in time a town grew up around the stream. The town was called Mecca. Abraham frequently visited his wife and child. Eventually, Abraham and Ismail built the Ka'ba together and embedded in it the Black Stone.

The stream, called Zamzam, flowed for thousands of years and continues to flow today. A well accessing the stream is enclosed in the Great Mosque in Mecca. People still drink from it and take bottles of the water home for their friends and relatives.

The first day of the Hajj is the Day of Reflection. Muslims reach Mecca and arrive at the Great Mosque. This mosque is gigantic! Its center courtyard can easily house a million people at one time. During the Hajj,

twice that number pack into it. The Ka'ba sits in this
courtyard, where the Hajj begins.

When the pilgrims arrive, they circle the Ka'ba seven
times. This *circumambulation* represents their lives re-
volving around God. It also represents the seven heavens,
which the Prophet Muhammad visited during his Night
Journey.

The Great Mosque is so huge that it encloses not only
the Ka'ba but also the Station of Abraham, the well of
Zamzam, and the two hills of Safa and Marwa. After
circumambulating the Ka'ba, pilgrims pray at the Station
of Abraham and then drink from the well of Zamzam.
They then walk seven times between the hills of Safa and
Marwa, to commemorate Hajar's running between these
two hills in her search for water.

The second day of Hajj is the Day of Standing.
Pilgrims travel to the Plain of Arafat, where Prophet
Muhammad delivered his farewell sermon before he died.
On this plain, Muslims pray and listen to sermons.

On the third day, the tenth of Dhu al-Hijja, the pilgrims travel to Mina, an ancient town nearby. Muslims
believe that Abraham passed through Mina on his way to
sacrifice Ismail. The devil himself appeared to Abraham
in Mina and tried to persuade him not to go through
with the sacrifice. Muslim tradition tells us that Abraham
threw stones at the devil to drive him away. It worked,
apparently, and the devil retreated. When modern-day
Muslim pilgrims reach Mina, they find three stone pillars

erected there, representing the devil. They throw stones at the pillars, which of course stay where they are.

The third day is also the day of Eid al-Adha, so pilgrims slaughter animals or arrange for someone else to do it, or they give charity in some other way. They then return to Mecca and repeat some of the rituals of the Hajj. On the fourth and fifth days, they return to Mina to repeat some rituals there, before returning to Mecca and ending the Hajj there on the twelfth day of Dhu al-Hijja.

After the end of the Hajj, many pilgrims travel to Medina to visit the Prophet's Mosque there. The Prophet's Mosque is much bigger than the structure that the Prophet Muhammad himself built. The new one holds a million worshipers and is about the size of the entire original city of Medina.

The Hajj is not easy. Pilgrims walk for miles, sleep in the open, and get pushed and shoved and jostled. Still, it's not so different from other religious pilgrimages. All involve traveling to a sacred place, performing certain rituals and prayers, and making some sort of spiritual connection. Traditionally, pilgrimages like the Hajj do involve some level of hardship. But if they were more convenient, they might not be so meaningful.

## Chapter 8

## Everyday Rules of Behavior for Muslims

Some actions are considered despicable by just about everybody. It doesn't matter if you belong to a religion or not—everyone knows there are certain things you should not do. Most of what Muslims should do or not do is the same as what people of other religions (or no religion) should do or not do. The rules of behavior in Islam have much in common with universal ideas of right and wrong.

For example, Muslims may not steal from or rob people. Muslims may not murder people or otherwise commit violence against them. Muslims may not lend money and then repeatedly increase the amount the borrower owes them. Muslims may not cheat people. These rules are consistent with universal notions of acceptable behavior.

So are some of the other rules. Muslims may not lie, for instance. Several verses of the Qur'an prohibit lying. For instance, one says, "Shun the word that is a lie."[1] Another says, "Do not confuse truth with falsehood, and do not knowingly lie."[2] Finally, the Qur'an warns, "Woe to every sinful liar."[3]

Being truthful is a universal value. Generations of American schoolchildren have heard the story of George Washington, who, enamored of his new axe, chopped down his father's cherry tree and then confessed to his father, saying, "I cannot tell a lie." This is often taught as a true story (though some say it was invented by Washington's biographer to illustrate Washington's honesty), and it shows how much we value honesty and truth.

Similarly, a famous Muslim story illustrates the importance of being honest. It's also said to be a true story.[4]

Abdul Qadir Jilani was born in 1077. As he grew up, he learned as much as he could, but he longed for more education than his village could give him. He dreamed of traveling to Baghdad (or "City of Peace"), which was an advanced center of civilization in the eleventh century. In Baghdad, at the *Bayt al-Hikmah* ("House of Wisdom"), he could attend classes and study with the best scholars— not only Muslim ones, but those of other religions, too.

By the time Abdul Qadir was eighteen years old, he and his mother had saved up enough money for his difficult journey to Baghdad. He planned to travel with a caravan. His mother sewed forty silver coins into the lining of his coat, to conceal them in case robbers attacked.

After a few days of travel, Abdul Qadir's caravan was indeed attacked by robbers. They stole valuable goods from the merchants traveling with the caravan, but they dismissed Abdul Qadir in his ragged coat, because he looked too poor. Still, just to be sure, they asked him, as they were turning to leave, "Do you have anything of value?"

"Well," said Abdul Qadir apologetically, "yes."

The robber leader turned back and burst out laughing. "You look too poor to own anything!" he scoffed. "What do you have?"

"I have forty dinars," replied Abdul Qadir, "sewn into my coat."

The robber leader patted Abdul Qadir's coat and found the jangling lump of coins sitting heavily in the lining. His expression changed.

"Why did you tell us?"asked the robber curiously. "We would have left and you would have kept your money."

"I promised my mother I would never lie to anyone. Even if you hadn't detected my lie, God would have known about it. I couldn't let that happen."

The robbers were so ashamed when they heard how honest and virtuous the young man was that they returned the goods and money they had stolen from the merchants. Abdul Qadir kept his forty dinars and reached Baghdad. There he became a famous scholar. His writings are still available today. The robbers, according to the story, reformed their ways and settled down to honest occupations.

Virtue and honesty do not always result in fairness and justice, as they do in this story. Good deeds are not always rewarded, and criminals are not always shamed into reforming. But this story does show how important honesty is in Islam, so much so that the tale has survived for a thousand years as an illustration of Islamic values.

Unfortunately, no religious group can claim that all of its members are honest. But Muslims are *supposed* to be truthful and honest, because Islam, along with other religions, values these traits.

Hypocrites are liars of a sort. Hypocrites are particularly despised in Islam because of certain events in history. Muhammad and his early followers were persecuted and even tortured because of their new religion, and attempts were made to assassinate Muhammad. On more than one occasion, he and his followers were betrayed by people who had pretended to be on his side. It made a deep impression on Muslims. Therefore, deception and hypocrisy, as well as lying, are forbidden in the Qur'an.

These are obvious principles that all religions have in common. But Islam has some less obvious prohibitions. For example, Muslims may not gamble.

Gambling means betting on a chance event. If the event comes to pass, you win. If the event does not come to pass, you lose. Usually, winning a bet means you gain money or a benefit, and losing a bet means you have to pay money or lose a benefit.

An example known to cultures all over the world is betting on dice. If you throw a pair of dice and say "I bet you a dollar that I get a seven when I throw the dice," that's betting on a chance event. It's considered gambling.

It would be easy to lose a lot of money by gambling. Many people have done so. That is why Islam prohibits it.

Gambling is different from simply taking a risk, which is allowed. Suppose you ask me to invest in an ice cream shop. That means I would pay you some money to start up your shop, and in return you would agree to pay me a part of what you earn from the store. You might say you will pay me one-quarter of the money you make, once people start understanding how wonderful your ice cream flavors are.

I may not know whether the ice cream store is going to succeed, and therefore I'm taking a risk with my money. But even so, this is not gambling, but *investing*—I am counting on your great idea and your hard work and not just on a chance event like an earthquake or whether the dice land on certain numbers. Investments are encouraged in Islam.

Now, suppose I invest in your shop, but things don't go well. We're disappointed to find that people do not like the ice cream. Suppose I get frustrated with the whole thing. If I start saying nasty things about you and your ice cream shop behind your back, I am violating Islamic principles. I'm not violating the gambling prohibition, but I *am* violating the Islamic rules that have to do with "backbiting."

In Islam, backbiting means making nasty statements behind someone's back. It's easy to do, sometimes, but the Qur'an clearly says that this is the wrong thing to do: "Do not pry into each other's secrets [spy on each other], nor backbite one another."[5]

The Qur'an defines other rules of good behavior as well. It adjures people to be kind and fair, to fulfill their promises, and to be patient.[6] The Qur'an also commands people to refrain from making fun of each other, defaming anyone (that is, not say anything about someone that is not true), and boasting.[7]

And finally, the Qur'an says that God loves those who "control their anger and are forgiving toward people."[8]

These rules of behavior are similar to those of other religions. Many religions have some version of the Golden Rule: "Do unto others as you would have them do unto you." In Islam, it is phrased this way, in a statement that Muhammad made: "None of you truly believes until you want for your brother what you want for yourself."

This refers to *all* people, not just men. The word "brother" is used here like the word "mankind" is used. It means, "None of you truly believes, until you want for other people what you want for yourself."

The Golden Rule is about compassion. Compassion is central to Islam, as it is to all religions. Virtually every chapter of the Qur'an begins with the statement "God is most compassionate, most forgiving."

The Qur'an also contains at least one other version of the Golden Rule (but remember that it's a translation of an ancient form of Arabic, so it might not sound like the Golden Rule in English). It goes like this: "Whoever performs a good deed, it is for himself, and whoever does wrong, it is against himself."[9]

This verse means that if you do good to others, it is like doing something good to yourself, and if you do something bad to others, it is like doing something bad to yourself.

A Christian concept related to the Golden Rule is that of "turning the other cheek." In the Qur'an, it's phrased this way: "Overlook others' failings with a gracious forgiveness."[10] One of the Muslim stories illustrating the importance of "turning the other cheek" features a religious teacher and scholar named Bayazid Bistami.[11]

Bayazid was born in what is now Iran, in the ninth century. Late one night, while walking home, Bayazid found a drunkard sprawled in the path, playing the lute. As Bayazid approached, the drunkard began to call him filthy names. Bayazid stepped around the man and did not answer. The drunkard grew more vicious in his insults, but Bayazid continued silently on his way. The drunkard, frustrated at the lack of response, ran after Bayazid and swung his lute down with a crash atop Bayazid's head! The lute shattered and fell in pieces all over the path. Staggering a little, Bayazid nevertheless did not turn his head or say a word. He continued on his way, dabbing at his bleeding face with his handkerchief.

The next day, Bayazid sent the drunkard a bag of coins and a dish of sweets, along with a note that read, "My head broke your lute last night. I apologize and offer this money so that you may replace it. And since your tongue last night was particularly bitter, please accept these desserts to sweeten it."

The drunkard, of course, was not following Islamic rules of behavior, as the Qur'an tells us not to insult people or call them derogatory names![12]

I'm certainly not saying all Muslims are able to follow all these rules all the time. Every religion has rules like these, which people *aspire* to follow. But being human sometimes gets in the way.

## Chapter 9

# Fashion Sense (or, What Muslims Wear)

*M*uslims wear all sorts of garments. Various kinds of clothes satisfy Islamic guidelines, which basically advise Muslims to dress modestly. There's really no such thing as "Muslim garb," or clothing that all Muslims wear.

I, along with the Muslims I grew up with, usually wore typical American clothes. To us, jeans and sweatshirts were just as "Islamic" as any other clothes, because they satisfied Islamic guidelines. Because I come from two cultures, American and Indian-Pakistani, I occasionally wore Indian-Pakistani clothing, but this was *cultural* clothing—not religious clothing.

"Cultural" or "ethnic" clothing, sometimes called "native" clothing, is clothing that comes from a particular country or geographical region. Such clothing does not necessarily come from religious requirements. For example, Scottish kilts are a form of cultural clothing. They are not a form of "Christian" clothing, because you do not have to wear them in order to be Christian, and you do not have to be Christian in order to wear them. Similarly, Indian-Pakistani clothing is not "Islamic" clothing but cultural clothing.

There is no particular kind of clothing that I must wear to be Muslim or that Islam says I must wear. Muslims from different countries wear clothing from their various cultures. Sometimes I see websites that advertise "Islamic clothing," but this is really just modest clothing that provides a lot of coverage for the body and that might be difficult to find in American department stores. It's usually full-length clothing with long sleeves and high necklines. These websites also sell head scarves.

What about head scarves, then? Is a head scarf "Islamic clothing"?

This is something on which Muslims disagree. Some Muslims believe Islam requires women to cover their hair, and some believe it does not. Growing up in the 1970s, I rarely saw Muslim women covering their hair. Most Muslim women in the world did not choose to cover their hair. Since then, the number has increased, but it's hard to estimate the numbers, because Muslim women who *don't* cover their hair aren't visually identifiable as Muslim.

Some of the women you might see with their heads

covered may not even be Muslim. That's because some
*non*-Muslim women cover their hair, too. These include
some Jewish women, some Rastafarian women, some
Hindu women, and some Catholic women. In many cultures, such as that of Greece, head scarves have long been
part of traditional cultural clothing. In addition, American girls and women occasionally wear head coverings,
such as bandanas, hoods, scarves, or knit hats.

Sometimes I see a picture of a woman in long black
billowing robes, wearing a face veil (*niqab*) showing only
her eyes. Occasionally I see a picture of a woman wearing
a *burqa*, which covers up everything, including the eyes,
which are hidden behind a panel of netting. These women
might look scary to us, because they look different; we
cannot see their facial expressions, and most of us are un-
accustomed to people covering their faces. These pictures
of veiled women are usually identified as Muslim
women—so, isn't this "Islamic dress"?

The great majority of Islamic scholars today do *not*
consider face veils to be Islamic. Rather, most Islamic
scholars consider face veils to be cultural dress, originating in certain countries in the Middle East. A prominent
Islamic scholar says that the niqab originated before the
birth of Islam, from a time when both men and women
wore it in the desert, and that it has no basis in the
Qur'an or the Sunnah.[1] (The Sunnah, discussed in
Chapter 13, is the words and deeds of Prophet Muhammad.) Only a tiny percentage of Muslim women worldwide wear face veils, but those women catch our attention.

Women are prohibited from wearing face veils in Mecca during the Hajj.

Syria and Egypt, which are both Muslim-majority countries, ban the face veil in university classrooms. Turkey, also a Muslim-majority country, bans face veils in government institutions (like public schools and government offices) and for decades also banned head scarves there. Some European countries, like France, have also banned the face veil in public, as well as the head scarf in government institutions.

Interestingly, Muslim women are not the only ones who cover themselves from head to toe. In parts of India, some non-Muslim women fully cover themselves, their scarves covering even their faces. In Israel, a very small minority of Jewish women wear the *sal*, a garment resembling the burqa and covering the face as well as the rest of the body.[2]

If there is no such thing as "Islamic clothing," then does Islam say *anything* about how people should dress? Yes, but it's subject to many different interpretations, and so not all Muslims agree on what it means.

The Qur'an, the Islamic holy book, contains more than 6,200 verses. Only three refer to clothing. These verses tell us that

- both men and women should be modest;
- both men and women should lower their gaze (that is, not leer at or ogle members of the opposite sex);
- both men and women should be chaste;

- people should not display parts of their bodies that wouldn't be decent to show;
- women should draw their head cloths over their chests to cover them; and
- women should draw their outer garments (such as cloaks or shawls) closely about them.

These verses do not specify *exactly* what people should wear but instead give general guidelines. Because these verses are not specific, Muslims have always debated their meaning, asking themselves: What clothing is modest and what isn't, according to the Qur'an? What does the Qur'an mean by "decent to show"? What does the Qur'an mean by "head cloth"?

To understand these debates, it's important to understand how people dressed in Arabia in the seventh century. At that time, women wore a piece of cloth that attached to the back of their heads and fell down their backs. Their tunics opened widely and often left their chests bare. Working women tended to be less covered than upper-class women, who sometimes wore veils as a sign of high status.

In their debates, the early Muslim scholars disagreed on many points, but they all agreed on some basics. They all agreed that both men and women had to cover their private parts, because it wouldn't be "decent to show" them. They all agreed that Muslim women had to cover their chests, because the Qur'an said so. In our modern times, we generally agree with these principles, in that we consider it decent to cover our chests and private parts.

Using these principles as a basis for more discussion, the early Muslims agreed on a few more aspects of dress. They all agreed that men had to be covered at least from their knees to their navels. And they all agreed that women had to be covered from their chests down to their knees.

But beyond these agreed-upon basics, there was disagreement. Most Muslim scholars, but not all, said that women should cover their heads. Very few said that women should cover their faces. They all agreed that women's chests had to be covered, but they disagreed on what exactly was meant by "chest"—did it start at the base of the neck, or lower down? Should a head scarf cover all the hair, or just some of it? Did the neck have to be covered? If hands, face, and feet could show, then did the definition of "hand" include the forearm, too? Did the definition of "feet" include the ankle? The calf? The scholars had different answers to these questions.[3]

Historically, Muslim women did not uniformly cover their hair. In early Islam, some women even prayed with their hair uncovered. Today, though, Muslim women do cover their hair while praying, whether or not they do so at other times.

The early Muslims considered several factors when interpreting the Qur'anic verses. Culture and hardship were two of those factors. In Arabian culture, as well as most cultures around the world at that time, people commonly wore head coverings of some sort; since it was the norm, it made sense that the early Muslims would have taken it for granted that people covered their hair. They took hardship into account, too, when they said that women who worked in the fields or did other physically difficult work did not have to cover themselves so much that their clothing would hamper them in their work.

Like the early Muslims, modern Muslims have different opinions on what constitutes Islamic dress. Recently, two of the most eminent, highly qualified, and respected Muslim religious scholars in Egypt publicly debated whether head covering was a religious duty for Muslim women. One scholar said it was; the other said it was not.

If I want to obey the rules of my religion, whose opinion should I follow? In Islam, when two learned and qualified Islamic scholars say different things, a Muslim can choose whom to follow. I choose to follow those scholars who say that head covering is not a religious requirement.

Nevertheless, if I lived in Iran, I would wear a head scarf in public because the *government* requires women to wear some sort of head covering. I would have to comply with the government's law, regardless of my personal religious view. Similarly, in most of Saudi Arabia, the custom of head covering is so strong (and in some places required) that I would want to cover my hair out of respect for the culture I was visiting. In most of the fifty-some Muslim-majority countries, though, women may choose whether to cover their heads or not.

But consider the other side of the coin. Suppose I decided to follow the scholars who said it was my religious duty to cover my hair. In most countries, I could choose to do so. Nevertheless, if I lived in France today, I would not be allowed to wear a head scarf to school or to a government job.

To sum up so far: we can define Islamic clothing as modest clothing, but exactly what "modest" means is open to interpretation.

A middle school student once asked me a question. She said, "I think girls and women who wear head scarves are trying not to fit in, don't you?"

We have all, at some point, thought about how to fit in. Women who choose to wear head scarves certainly might prefer to fit in, but they might consider the head scarf to be a religious requirement and therefore more important than fitting in. Perhaps they are simply trying to be themselves.

I once heard a high school teacher describe an experiment she conducted.[4] She hung, in front of her classroom, a picture of a nun wearing a head covering. She then asked her students to write down the words that came into their minds as they gazed at the picture. The students wrote words like "holy," "pure," "chaste," and "faithful to God."

The teacher then replaced the picture with one of a

Middle Eastern woman wearing a head covering. Again the teacher asked her students to write down words that came to mind. The students, this time, wrote "stupid," "backward," and "oppressed."

The amount of covering was the same in both pictures. In the two pictures, the coverings were similar in color as well. Why were the students' reactions different?

Sometimes, head scarves are referred to as "symbols of Islam." They are simply a way of being modest, like choosing to wear long sleeves instead of short sleeves. I doubt anyone would say that long sleeves are a "symbol of Islam."

Muslim women's head coverings also vary in style. Some women wear colorful turbans. Some wear scarves with the front of their hair showing. Some wear loose scarves that cover the neck as well as the hair. Some wear *chadors*, which are Persian in origin, similar to robes and usually black, that leave only the face and hands showing.

Most Muslim women who cover their hair do so because they believe it's their religious duty. But three American Muslim women I know wear the head scarf for reasons other than religious duty. One tells me that she does *not* think hair covering is required, but it reminds her to do good things and be on her best behavior. The second woman grew up not wearing a head scarf; she decided to wear one to show other Americans that Muslims can be normal, professional, intelligent people (like her).

And the third says that, although she has not heard a good argument for covering her hair, she would rather err on the safe side.

For thousands of years, human beings have worn all sorts of coverings on their heads. In American movies from the first half of the twentieth century, women almost always wore hats or scarves when they went out in public, just as men usually wore hats. Women also sometimes wore fashionable turbans. We do not think of these movie stars as oppressed, even if they covered their hair, because they *chose* to do so. They had cultural reasons, not religious ones. However, does the reason matter if women have free choice about their dress? The vast majority of Muslim women do make free choices.

Dress codes in Islam were meant to be personal religious guidelines, not laws. The Prophet Muhammad never forced women to cover their hair. The scholars who developed the dress codes in Muslim tradition did not consider compliance to be mandatory in the way that prayer or fasting is considered mandatory. Rather, dress codes were a matter of "should do" rather than "must do."

The Islamic guidelines on dress were meant to apply to adults, not children. They were meant to apply only after puberty, and even then there was not unanimous agreement on them.

Even though today Muslims and non-Muslims alike seem to fixate on Muslim women's dress, rules on clothing were historically developed for reasons of modesty and protection. Dress codes were not about either oppression or freedom, any more than school dress codes are. The historical debates focused on the question of what was decent attire for men as well as women, usually in the context of prayer. The early Muslim scholars also understood that these rules were flexible, because cultural factors like custom and hardship are subject to change over centuries. Ultimately, Muslim fashion should be an individual choice.

Chapter 10

# Relationships Between Men and Women (or, Can I Go to the School Dance?)

Although men and women have danced together as couples for centuries in Western cultures, this practice is an alien concept in some non-Western cultures. In India, at the time my parents were growing up, a man and a woman did not dance together as a couple, no matter what their religion. In all the Indian movies I watched as a child, any dancing involved either one woman performing a dance or groups of young women dancing together in choreographed dances. Never did a man ask a woman to dance, lead her to a dance floor, and dance with her as a couple, à la Ginger Rogers and Fred Astaire (in 1930s movies) or Edward and Bella in *Twilight*. This cultural difference is illustrated in the

American musical *The King and I,* in which the English governess has to teach the waltz to the King of Siam (Thailand), because in his culture couples do not dance together.

In the United States, middle school dances are a part of growing up. But I, as an American Muslim girl, never attended school dances. I didn't go on dates or have a boyfriend. The reason for this was my family's interpretation of how I should practice my religion.

Islam, like most traditional religions, disapproves of physical relations between unmarried people. Therefore, Muslims should avoid situations that might lead to physical relations between unmarried people. For example, according to traditional religious guidelines, an unmarried and unrelated man and woman should avoid being together alone behind closed doors.

This traditional religious attitude is similar to the customs in many countries worldwide. Even in Western countries just over a hundred years ago, it was not considered suitable for a young woman to go out with a man unchaperoned, and if a young man visited a young woman in her home, the door to the room was left open. Things have changed, but the reasons behind both these Western rules and Islamic rules are essentially the same: to prevent difficult situations and to prevent men from taking advantage of women (or vice versa).

How does this relate to school dances? In my school, a girl attended a dance "with a boy." As in, "on a date." Usually, a boy had to ask a girl to dance with him. A dance was associated with romance. And since my parents thought it best to avoid romantic situations, I never went to a dance. Neither did most of my Muslim friends.

I had a few Muslim girlfriends, though, who did. They danced with other girls or in groups. A few of my Muslim friends attended dances with boys, but boys who understood that they were going "as friends." And it wasn't just my Muslim friends who were restricted; I had one Hindu friend who did not date because of her family's Hindu traditions.

At my daughter's school dances, however, students are not separated into couples. Everyone just shows up and dances in one big mass of humanity. Parents chaperone on the sidelines. At these dances, there's no romantic sense of boy-girl couples "going to the dance" together.

Given how school dances differ and how cultural and religious interpretations differ, you may come across a variety of Muslim behavior. You may know some Muslim classmates who absolutely do not attend dances no matter what, some who find nothing wrong with school dances, and some who fall somewhere in between. Yet they could all be complying with their interpretation of Islamic principles.

A small minority of Muslims believe that Islam requires as much segregation of men and women as possible. For example, shopping centers in Saudi Arabia are separated into different areas for single men and for single women. However, in Saudi Arabia an extreme interpretation of Islam is implemented, one that's not the norm in other Muslim countries. Islam itself has no rules saying that men and women can never interact.

In fact, the Prophet Muhammad himself did not segregate men and women. Women rode into battle with him. He consulted women and valued their advice. Women consulted with him, too.

In America, Muslims lead mixed-gender lives. We go to coed schools and work in coed workplaces. My parents trusted me to exercise good judgment and avoid situations where I could get into trouble with boys.

Good judgment means different things to different people, Muslim or otherwise. My Muslim friends and I reached different conclusions on the question of school dances. Another issue we all had to deal with was dating.

Again, because Muslims should avoid situations that could lead to physical relations outside of marriage, dating is often disapproved of or disallowed. However, the definition of dating may vary—that is, some Muslims may consider meeting at a restaurant for lunch to be a forbidden "date" and some may consider it perfectly allowable. Sometimes, it could depend upon whether the meeting was *intended* to be romantic or not. And some Muslims may consider dating to be perfectly permissible, as long as the rules prohibiting physical relations are observed.

Going out in groups is a common solution. In many countries, Muslim college students socialize in mixed-gender groups. They want to get to know one another, but also to observe Islamic guidelines. The restrictions on dating do not mean that Muslims cannot be friends with people of the opposite gender.

Even when Muslim men and women start looking for someone they might like to marry, the Islamic guidelines about physical relations outside marriage do not change. No matter how old men and women get, Islam prohibits physical relations outside marriage. This is based on verses in the Qur'an.

I was often asked how Muslims get married if they do not date. I met my husband at my summer job one year while I was in law school; we got to know each other primarily while talking on the telephone. Muslims might meet their future spouses at work or in class or through mutual friends. In some Muslim families, marriages are arranged by the parents. I don't mean "arranged" in the sense that the bride and groom meet for the first time at their wedding. But often the parents arrange for the potential bride and groom to meet and get to know each other. If they like each other, they marry.

Islamic guidelines concerning physical relations, however they are interpreted, apply to both men and women. Neither my brother nor I was allowed to date. To my surprise, many of my non-Muslim friends thought it reasonable that I, as a girl, didn't date but thought it shocking that my brother didn't!

Restrictions on male-female interactions may come from religion, culture, notions of modesty and chastity, personal comfort levels, or all of these. I see many of the same restrictions in some non-Muslim families that I see in Muslim families. Islamic guidelines may seem strict in today's society, but they do not prevent the vast majority of Muslims from participating in their schools or jobs or community.

## Part II

# When Did Islam Start and How Did It Develop?

*Chapter 11*

## Muhammad and His Mission

Muhammad is said to be the most popular boy's name in the world. In India, parents often name their boys Muhammad, which means "Praiseworthy." However, the boys are then called by their middle names rather than by Muhammad, which is treated as an honorific. The name Mary is sometimes used in the same way by Christians.

I, like Muslim children everywhere, grew up with stories of the Prophet. When I hated school in fifth grade and refused to go, my mother smiled at my mutinous face and said, "Remember, the Prophet said to pursue knowledge, even if you have to go all the way to China." (China seemed a world away from Arabia in the seventh century;

the Prophet was making a point about the importance of knowledge.) When I procrastinated about doing my homework, my father said, "Remember the first command God gave Muhammad? It was 'Read.'"

So the Prophet is not just a historical figure to Muslims; his wisdom is something we are all supposed to follow. But who was he? How did he become a prophet?

Muhammad was born sometime around 570 CE, in the city of Mecca, in what is now the country of Saudi Arabia. Mecca was located in a part of the Arabian peninsula called the Hijaz. Muhammad preached about universal goals, like fairness and justice, but he also often criticized the specific cultural practices of his own time. He tried to change the injustices around him through his preaching. Before we examine what exactly he preached, it's useful to know about the injustices he was preaching against.

At the time of Muhammad's birth, the settlement nearest Mecca was called Yathrib. Arabs who did not live in settlements were *nomadic*—that is, they moved their possessions around with them and did not confine themselves to one particular geographic area. Most Arabs at that time practiced a pagan, polytheistic religion. But Jewish and Christian Arabs, as well as other monotheistic Arabs, also lived in the area. In fact, some of Muhammad's relatives were pagan and some were Christian.

The seventh-century world anywhere was not a good place for women's rights, and Mecca was no exception. A woman could not divorce her husband. A man could have as many wives as he wanted; this practice of *polygyny* was common among Jewish Arabs as well as pagan Arabs, though not Christian Arabs. In seventh-century Arabia, a man could simply send his wife away when he no longer wanted her, while he kept any children. A woman could be sold into marriage by her male relatives. A woman could not enter into a contract on her own or testify in court. These restrictions on women were not, at that time, unique to Arabs; some or all of them were common to many cultures all over the world in the seventh century.

No police force existed in those days, in Arabia or anywhere else. There was no central government, either. If you were an Arab living in the seventh century, your clan—your family group within your tribe—protected you. The more powerful your clan and tribe, the better you were protected.

The wealthier the tribe, the more power it wielded. Tribes increased their wealth, in part, by raiding other tribes. This was considered acceptable, as long as no one was killed. Killing someone provoked a blood feud, in which the victim's tribe retaliated against the other tribe, which then retaliated by killing more people of the victim's tribe, and so on, for years.

Constant warfare was the norm. Only once a year was warfare halted—at the time of the pilgrimage and annual poetry festival in Mecca! I always imagine crowds of fierce desert warriors rushing around raiding each other's tribes, when suddenly someone calls out, "Hey, wait! Today's the beginning of the annual *poetry* festival!"—whereupon they all fling down their weapons and surge back to Mecca to listen to poetry.

This was the society into which Muhammad was born. Even as a young man, before he began to preach, Muhammad sought ways to address the injustices he saw. Before he was a prophet, he was a social reformer.

Muhammad was born into the *Banu Hashim* clan of the *Quraysh* tribe. When he was orphaned at the age of six, his paternal grandfather became his guardian. Upon his grandfather's death, Muhammad's paternal uncle became the head of his clan and his new guardian.

Muhammad received no formal schooling; in those days they didn't have a school system for everyone. Muslim tradition says Muhammad was illiterate; even if he could read and write, it would have been at a minimal level. Seventh-century Arabs were typical of many people in the world, in that they did not have books or magazines or other printed materials to read, as we do today. Stories and poetry were transmitted orally and memorized verbatim. This was before the printing press, so books could not be mass-produced and were valuable.

Upon reaching adulthood, Muhammad began working as a merchant. He established a reputation for himself as honest and trustworthy, and he soon obtained a position as a business manager for a beautiful widow, Khadija. Impressed with his honesty and integrity, she proposed marriage to him when he was twenty-five, and he accepted. She was forty years old, and they were married for nearly a quarter of a century, until her death. Muhammad defied the custom of the time by never taking another wife during his marriage to Khadija.

According to Muslim tradition, one night around the year 610, Muhammad retreated to a cave in the nearby mountains to meditate, as he often did. He did not realize, though, that this particular night would later be known as the Night of Power and would change the religious makeup of the world forever. For as Muhammad sat meditating in the isolated darkness of the cave, a sudden reverberating voice shattered the air around him.

"Read!" the voice commanded. (The command can also be translated as "Recite!")

Unseen arms pressed suffocatingly on Muhammad from every side. Terrified and struggling to breathe, Muhammad gasped out a reply.

"I cannot read!" he replied to the darkness.

But once more the ringing voice erupted from the depths of the cave.

"Read!" cried the voice.

"I do not know how!" Muhammad gasped.

And again, unseen arms squeezed his chest, compressing his lungs. A third time, the voice commanded, "Read!"

Despairing, Muhammad asked this time, "What shall I read?"

And from the listening darkness, he received this answer, which would become part of Surah 96, the first to be revealed, of the Qur'an:

*Read! In the name of your Lord who created,*
*Created mankind from a clot of blood!*
*Read! Your Lord is the Most Generous,*
*Who taught by the Pen,*
*Taught man what he knew not.*[1]

Muhammad shook with terror, shock, and doubt. Whose was the voice? A demon's?

An angel's. Or so Muslims believe. Muslims believe that the angel Gabriel visited Muhammad and brought these words to him from God. Gabriel would continue to bring God's words to Muhammad throughout his life. Muhammad recited the words aloud as he received them, and his followers wrote them down on whatever materials were available. Within twenty years after Muhammad's death, these words were collected and compiled into one book, the Qur'an.

But after this first encounter with the angel Gabriel, Muhammad stumbled home, shaken and shivering. He confided everything to his wife, Khadija. Upon hearing his story, Khadija promptly assured her husband that she believed him. She took Muhammad to consult her Christian cousin, Waraqa, a pious man who listened to Muhammad's fantastical story and reassured him that he must be a prophet of God.

Every year, on the anniversary of the Night of Power, the night that Muhammad received his first revelation from God, Muslims stay awake all night, praying and meditating. Muslim tradition says that God's presence fills the earth most intensely on this night and that it is possible to understand the speech of animals and hear the whispering of trees. Muslims believe that their prayers will more likely be granted on this night than on any other night of the year.

That very first Night of Power launched what would become the world's second-largest religion. After that night, Muhammad began preaching the glory of the One God. He saw himself as preaching not a new religion, but the religion of Abraham—the belief in one God.

As Muhammad became more successful in his preaching, the people of Mecca began to resent him. They persecuted him and his followers. The Meccans resented him less for his new religion (of which there were several in the Hijaz already) than for overturning their social structure. Muhammad did this in several ways.

First, people converted to Islam as individuals, not as clans. Islam did not recognize any hierarchy among people—that is, Muslims were considered equal, no matter what their clan, tribe, or race. That meant that Islam blurred class distinctions. Suddenly, lower classes were considered equal to upper classes. The upper classes didn't like this.

In the chapter on prayer, I mentioned Bilal, the first muezzin of Islam. Not only did he have dark skin, he was a freed Ethopian slave. Yet Muhammad gave him the exalted honor of being the first muezzin. This was the sort of action that caused resentment among upper-class Meccans.

Second, Muhammad's religion affected the business structure of Mecca. The Ka'ba was in Mecca, and it was an ancient site of pilgrimage. In Muhammad's time, the Ka'ba was filled with idols, which people traveled from afar to worship. This was good for Mecca's business, as visitors and pilgrims bought goods from Meccan merchants.

Muhammad's religion of the One God undermined the polytheistic religion and its idols. Muhammad believed that Abraham and Ismail had built the Ka'ba for the worship of the One God, but that, over time, Abraham's message had been forgotten and the Arabs had begun worshiping idols instead of God. For the Meccans, undermining the idols was bad for business.

Third, the Meccans believed that Muhammad gave too many rights to women. Under Islam, women could divorce their husbands under certain conditions. They could keep their young children in case of divorce. They were given a required share of inheritance. They could enter into their own contracts. They could testify in court. They could not be sold into marriage. These changes were extremely feminist and progressive for the seventh century, anywhere in the world, and they didn't go over well in *patriarchal* (male-dominated) societies like Mecca.

Fourth, Muhammad preached on behalf of the disadvantaged. He told the Meccans to care for widows, orphans, disabled people, and poor people. But Meccan society was based on the idea that the *tribes* were responsible for their members. If an orphan's tribe was not powerful, or if he had no tribe, then it was too bad—why should other Meccans have to care for him?

Muhammad also forbade untruthful contracts and *usury*. A common practice at the time involved lending money to a borrower and then doubling the amount the borrower owed if he could not pay it back on the due date. This was usury; so was charging huge fees for borrowing money and huge penalties for not being able to pay the money back. Such practices benefited the wealthy and were a matter of life or death for the poor.

Throughout history, those who have preached new religions have often been resented, because they have frequently introduced unwelcome ideas. Muhammad's ideas were unwelcome to the Meccans.

"He must be stopped," the Meccans said, "before he destroys our society."

The Meccans began to persecute Muhammad and his followers, using torture, exile, and harassment. A group of Muhammad's followers fled to Abyssinia (now Ethiopia), where the Christian king welcomed them. Muhammad stayed in Mecca.

In 619, Khadija and Muhammad's uncle both died. Although his uncle had never converted to Muhammad's religion, he had loved Muhammad and protected him. The new head of the Banu Hashim hated Muhammad and formally withdrew his protection. As a result, Muhammad faced assassination.

Because of the danger, Muhammad and his followers

searched for a new home. Eventually Muhammad received an invitation from leaders of the nearby city of Yathrib, which was plagued by a feud between two large pagan tribes. The feud was growing so large that the other citizens of the city (pagans, Jews, and Christians) had begun to take sides. They needed a disinterested outsider to keep the peace. They invited Muhammad, because they knew he needed a home and he had a reputation for honesty.

Secretly, Muhammad and his followers trickled away in small groups from Mecca to Yathrib. They numbered less than one hundred. The year was 622, and the Islamic calendar starts from this year, the year of the *Hijra,* or "Migration."

Muhammad's new "job" was as a *hakam,* or an arbiter. This is someone who listens to all sides of the argument and then either decides who is correct or finds a solution to the problem. Muhammad was the religious leader of only his Muslim followers. The pagan tribes and the Jews kept their religious practices, but pledged to follow Muhammad's political leadership and help each other defend the city in case of attack. They did not become members of Muhammad's religious group unless they wanted to.

In Yathrib, the number of Muhammad's followers grew, and eventually he became the political leader of the city, as well as religious leader of the Muslims. The name of the city was changed from Yathrib to *Medinat an-Nabi,* or "City of the Prophet." It was called *Medina* for short.

Medina was a city in which all the inhabitants were

politically allied and committed to defending themselves from outside attack, but free to abide by their own religious laws. The people of Medina eventually entered into a contract, the Constitution of Medina. Muslims believe that the Constitution of Medina is the first charter (political agreement) of religious freedom in the world.

During his years in Medina, the Meccans remained Muhammad's enemies. Muhammad wanted to win the Meccans over to his cause, but not by killing them or converting them at sword point. To Muhammad, it was crucial that Mecca and Medina become willing partners and not competitors.

Why did Muhammad care about Mecca? He was Meccan himself, and Mecca had been his home. In addition, Medina was competing with Mecca for local resources and trade; it would be better if they were allies rather than enemies. Perhaps most importantly, the Ka'ba was in Mecca.

The Ka'ba was very important to Muhammad. The Qur'an had told Muslims to face the Ka'ba when praying. In addition, Muslims believed Abraham had built the Ka'ba for the worship of the One God. Arabs from all over the region came to the Ka'ba for pilgrimage. It was a powerful symbol. Muhammad believed that it was his duty to restore the Ka'ba to its rightful role. But he wanted to carry out this duty without bloodshed, because the Qur'an forbids any warfare that is not in self-defense (more on this in Chapter 14).

How could Muhammad get the Meccans on his side

without fighting? They had persecuted him in Mecca and were unlikely to want his friendship. The first step was to get their attention.

Muhammad sent his followers off to raid tribal caravans traveling to and from Mecca. This would be stealing in today's world, but in seventh-century Arabia, it was an acceptable, legal activity, as long as no one was hurt. Acceptable though it was, it was nevertheless irritating and inconvenient for the Meccans, and they got tired of it. They resorted to armed combat. The next time Muhammad ventured outside Medina to raid a caravan, he was met by a Meccan army of a thousand warriors.

Despite being outnumbered, the Muslims won the first battle, the Battle of Badr. They lost the second, the Battle of Uhud, with heavy losses. The third time the Meccans attacked, with an army of ten thousand, Muhammad's followers dug a huge ditch, or trench, around the city of Medina. The Meccan army could not cross it and eventually retreated back to Mecca.

What Muhammad had accomplished was show the Meccans, whose society was based on strength and warfare, that he deserved respect and would fight to defend his followers. He had shown them that he was no longer simply a refugee they had driven out of Mecca, but someone the Meccans had to deal with as an equal. The battles and the tribal raiding opened the door for negotiations.

In 628, Muhammad decided to make his pilgrimage to the Ka'ba. The Ka'ba had always been open to everyone. He set off for the Ka'ba with approximately fifteen hundred of his followers.

The Meccans interpreted this move as hostile, despite the fact that the Muslims were unarmed and wearing their white pilgrim's clothing. Messengers intercepted Muhammad with the message that he would not be allowed to make his pilgrimage to Mecca.

After some negotiations, the Meccans and the Muslims signed a peace treaty, the Treaty of al-Hudaybiyyah. In the treaty, they agreed to refrain from warfare for ten years. The treaty also forbade the Muslims from continuing to the Ka'ba, but allowed them to come back the following year.

Some of Muhammad's followers were incensed. The Ka'ba was supposed to be open to everyone! They considered it their right to make the pilgrimage. But Muhammad signed the treaty and went home.

The next year, Muhammad returned to make his pilgrimage. The Meccans were surprised by the respect he and his followers showed for the Ka'ba. After a peaceful pilgrimage, Muhammad and his followers returned to Medina.

But within two years of the peace treaty, war broke out again. A tribe affiliated with the Quraysh (the dominant Meccan tribe) attacked a tribe loyal to Muhammad. Responding decisively, Muhammad gathered an army and marched toward Mecca.

The Meccans at this point were uncomfortable. They

knew they had broken the treaty. They were demoralized because of the number of people who had joined Muhammad and his new religion. Muhammad was now a significant political leader, and by the rules of that time, they had wronged him by breaking the treaty. So they surrendered without a fight.

The Meccans sent a messenger to intercept Muhammad, who agreed to their surrender. In those days in Arabia, and in much of the world, when one side triumphed in warfare, the losing side did not simply go home. The men were typically executed and the women and children were enslaved. This was the custom throughout the Arabian peninsula, as well as elsewhere, regardless of religion.

Yet when Mecca surrendered, Muhammad declared a general amnesty (a forgiveness of all past offenses) for everyone who laid down his weapons. Muhammad pardoned even people who had killed members of his own family. The only act of destruction he undertook was that of the stone idols in the Ka'ba. He rededicated the Ka'ba to the worship of one God.

Muhammad never converted people to his cause by force. Instead, he famously challenged his followers, "Will you then force men to believe when belief can come only from God?"[2] Muhammad did fight for his people, and he did engage in military combat, but he never started a war and never fought when he could negotiate instead. He followed the rules of war and politics used by everyone else in the region at that time, including Jews and pagan Arabs. And on many occasions, he did not exercise his customary rights, choosing instead to retreat or forgive. Sometimes, for this very reason, his followers criticized him for being weak.

Twenty days after the surrender of Mecca in 630, Muhammad returned to Medina. He was not to live long afterward. In 632, he set out once more to make his pilgrimage to the Ka'ba. It was to be his last.

At the conclusion of this pilgrimage, Muhammad gave his last sermon. Called the "Farewell Sermon," it has been quoted for nearly fourteen hundred years. Shortly after his Farewell Sermon, Muhammad returned to Medina, where he became ill and died. He was sixty-three years old.

*Chapter 12*

# How Muslims View the World: God, Angels, and Adam and Eve

The angel Gabriel is a supporting actor in both the Christian and the Islamic religious traditions. Gabriel is common to the two religions because Islam accepts Judaism and Christianity as part of its own tradition. Just as Christianity accepts Judaism, with some changes, as part of itself, Islam accepts both Judaism and Christianity, with some changes, as part of Islam. Muslims believe in the story of Adam and Eve. Muslims accept the Judeo-Christian prophets, including Noah, Abraham, Solomon, David, Moses, Jesus, and many others. In fact, the Qur'an states that God has sent a prophet to *every* community of people throughout history—thousands of them. This is why some Muslims (but not most) accept prophets and religious texts from non-Judeo-Christian traditions as well.

Muslims believe in God, heaven, hell, an afterlife, angels (which are neither male nor female in Islam), and the devil (as the former angel who, back-talking and belligerent, was expelled from heaven). We believe that people will be held accountable for their deeds after they die. Muslims believe that accountability goes into effect on the Day of Judgment, when all souls will answer for what they have done in their lives.

Although Islam accepts the Judeo-Christian prophets, sometimes the stories about them differ. Muslims believe that all the prophets were human and not divine. Therefore, we believe that Muhammad was a human being, albeit one who received God's message.

In the same way, Muslims believe that Jesus was a human prophet, not the son of God. Muslims have great respect for Jesus, though, as well as for Moses; Jesus and Moses are two of the most important prophets in Islam. Muslims also believe in Mary, the mother of Jesus. The Qur'an contains an entire chapter (Surah 19) named after her.

According to Muslim tradition, Mary was chosen by God because she was virtuous and pure. Islam accepts the virgin birth of Jesus. Muslims believe that God simply willed Jesus into being and sent an angel to tell Mary that she would bear a son. Astonished, Mary asked how she could possibly have a son when no man had touched her. The angel smiled indulgently and replied:

> *Thus it will be.*
> *Your Lord has said, "It is easy for Me"*
> *And that "We shall make him a sign for men*
> *And a blessing from Us."*
> *This is a thing already decreed.*[1]

This Qur'anic verse says that God made Jesus as a "sign for men" and a "blessing" from God. After that, Mary gave birth to him.

Muslims believe that Jesus did not actually die on the cross, but that he was raised up to God, who made it only *appear* that Jesus had died after informing him that his term was coming to an end. Although Jesus's story is different in Islam, this does not diminish Muslim respect for Jesus.

Muslims also believe in Adam and Eve as the "parents" of humankind. Muslims revere Adam as the first prophet. Here's the Islamic version of the creation story:

Adam and Eve first resided in heaven, where they were perfectly happy. They were respected—all the angels except one had bowed to Adam upon his creation—and they had no worries. The only impediment to their complete contentment was that God had forbidden them to eat the fruit of a certain tree. Just a small restriction. But it was enough.

Satan, duplicitous and insidious, crept furtively into

the garden of heaven, revenge on his mind. He had been kicked out of heaven for disobeying God and not bowing to Adam. And who *was* Adam, anyway, to get him exiled from heaven? A soft, powerless being, in Satan's opinion.

Satan appeared to Adam and tried to tempt him (not Eve) to eat the forbidden fruit.[2] Unfortunately, from Adam's point of view, Satan succeeded in his mission of revenge. In the end, both Adam and Eve ate the fruit and found themselves in deep, deep trouble with God.

Because they had disobeyed God, Adam and Eve were expelled from heaven. They asked for God's forgiveness, though, and God did forgive them, to Satan's disgust. God promised them guidance and told them that if they behaved well, they and their descendants could come back to heaven.

Islam has no concept of original sin. In the Islamic view, Adam and Eve disobeyed God but were forgiven. Their descendants do not inherit their sin.

Muslims believe that individuals are responsible for their actions; if they sin, they can repent and ask for forgiveness. Virtually every chapter of the Qur'an begins with the words "God is most compassionate, most forgiving," and many verses speak of God's mercy. Muslims believe that all people will account for their deeds on the Day of Judgment.

Muslims believe that all people, whatever their race or religion, are descended from Adam and Eve. According to Islam, anyone performing good deeds, *including non-Muslims,* will go to heaven. In other words, under

Islamic law, a person need not be Muslim to go to heaven. The Qur'an says:

"The Muslims, the Jews, the Christians, and the Sabians, *any* who believe in God and the last day and do good, have their reward with their Lord. There is nothing for them to fear; they will not sorrow."[3]

Jews, Christians, and Sabians are examples of religious groups called, in Islam, "People of an Earlier Revelation"— that is, people who received an earlier "revelation," or "message," from God. Frequently, this term is translated as "People of the Book"; but "Book" in this phrase doesn't mean a physical book you can hold in your hand. Rather, it refers to the "Book of God," or "God's Word," which are synonyms for "God's message." Put another way, "People of the Book" means "People Who Have Already Received God's Message."

People of an Earlier Revelation are particularly respected in Islam, as you can see in the verse above. As Islam spread and Muslims encountered other religious groups like Hindus, Zoroastrians, and Buddhists, the definition of "People of an Earlier Revelation" expanded to include them, too.

If the Adam and Eve story describes how humankind was created by God, then where does evolutionary theory fit into Islam? Evolutionary theory is a scientific theory that says, essentially, that all species evolve over time. According to evolutionary theory, human beings evolved over tens of thousands of years, from primitive primates into more advanced primates into current human beings.

In other words, evolutionary theory says, we human beings were not made fully fledged in our current forms—
rather, we developed *into* them.

Evolutionary theory also indicates that humans share
a common ancestor with chimpanzees and gorillas.
In fact, we now know that we share 96 percent of our
*genome*—which is our entire set of genetic material—
with chimpanzees. Despite the shock this discovery originally caused, evolutionary theory is now widely accepted
in the scientific community.

But what about the religious community? Does evolutionary theory conflict with the story of Adam and Eve?
If we evolved from primitive beings, does not that conflict with the creation story, which portrays Adam and
Eve as humans like us?

Some Muslims, like some Christians and some Jews,
do not accept evolutionary theory for this very reason,
that it conflicts with the creation story. But other Muslims believe that Islam and evolutionary theory can be
reconciled.

The Qur'an is not always meant to be taken literally.
Qur'anic stories are sometimes metaphors. For example,
the Qur'an does say that creation took six days. This
might at first seem to contradict evolutionary theory,
which indicates that humans took thousands of years to
evolve. But the Qur'an also says that one of God's days
might be a thousand, or even fifty thousand, of our own
days. The creation story may be a metaphorical, rather
than a literal, description of creation. The Qur'an was

addressing an ancient, seventh-century civilization, which was not advanced in biology. The Qur'an spoke to the people of that time in a way they would understand.

Other aspects of the creation story and evolution can be reconciled, too, but I want to emphasize again that not all Muslims would agree with this reconciliation of religion and evolutionary theory, just as not all Christians and Jews would. Polls show that the percentage of Muslim Americans who believe in evolution is about the same as the percentage of all Americans who believe in evolution.[4]

So far, the Islamic worldview has been similar to the Judeo-Christian one. However, the Islamic worldview includes one type of character not included in the Judeo-Christian tradition. These are the *jinn,* beings that sound just a bit like something from *Star Trek.*

Arabs living in Arabia before Islam believed the jinn to be unseen beings. The Arabs thought of them as elemental spirits, and they were featured in Arabic folktales the way elves and leprechauns are featured in Western folktales. The Western notion of a "genie" in a lamp, ready to grant you three wishes, comes from translations of Arabic folktales, such as those collected in *The Thousand and One Nights.*

The folktale version of a jinn (or genie) has little to do with the Qur'anic version of jinn. The Qur'an confirms the existence of jinn, but says little else about them. "Jinn" has several possible meanings in the Qur'an, mostly referring to beings that are outside of our perception—that is, beings we cannot sense.

In the seventh century, this Qur'anic definition could have applied to germs and single-celled organisms, since these were beings outside of people's perceptions at the time (no microscopes back then). The word "jinn," as used in the Qur'an, may also refer to certain forces of nature or unseen forces, like gravity or radiation. The Qur'an was advising seventh-century people of things beyond their knowledge and perception.

Nevertheless, some Muslims do equate the Qur'anic jinn with the jinn of folklore. They conceive of jinn as closer to the colorful jinn of Arabic folklore. This is not too different from how, in every culture, some people believe in the supernatural and some do not.

*Chapter 13*

# The Basis of Islam:
# The Qur'an, the Sunnah, and the Shariah

## The Qur'an

The word "Qur'an" means "Recitation." The Qur'an is, in fact, a compilation of Muhammad's recitations. Muslims believe that these recitations are God's exact words, brought to Muhammad by the angel Gabriel. In another sense, the Qur'an is a recitation because it is meant to be recited aloud. It has a rhythm and cadence you cannot hear otherwise. Muslims recite the Qur'an during prayer, formal recitals, in recordings, and in Qur'an-reciting contests. Qur'an reciting is considered an art form.

How is "Qur'an" pronounced? The apostrophe in

"Qur'an" represents a slight *stop*, or pause, in the sound of the word. We make the same kind of pause when we say "uh-oh." We stop for a fraction of a second between the "uh" and the "oh." The hyphen in "uh-oh" works the same way the apostrophe in "Qur'an" does. There's a fractional stop after the "Qur" and before the "an."

The *Q* sound in "Qur'an" is different from a *k* sound. It is more guttural, originating from deep in the throat, rather than from the mouth. To make this sound, cover your throat with the back of your tongue and lift your tongue up (opening your throat) at the same time you emit a sound. That sound should be the Arabic *q* sound.

The Qur'an can be frustrating to read, because it does not read like a story. It reads more like a series of poems in unmetered verse. Muslims think of it as "an outpouring of divine messages."[1]

Sometimes, these Qur'anic messages can seem unconnected and disjointed. This is partly because the Qur'an was not organized in chronological order, the order in which Muhammad received it. Instead, the Qur'an is organized generally by chapter length.

The Qur'an consists of 114 *surahs*, or chapters. The lines (or verses) making up each surah are called *ayahs*. Generally, the longest surahs are at the beginning of the Qur'an, and the shortest surahs are at the end.

One exception to this general rule is the first surah, called *al-Fatiha*, or "The Opening." This surah is recited more often than any other; it encapsulates the spirit and many of the ideas in the Qur'an. Here is one translation of al-Fatiha, based on Michael Sells's version from *Approaching the Qur'an:*

> In the name of God,
>    The Compassionate, the Forgiving.
> Praise be to God,
>    Lord of all the worlds,
>    The Compassionate, the Forgiving,
>    Master of the Day of Judgment.
> To you we turn in worship,
>    And to you we turn in time of need.
> Guide us to the straight road,
>    The road of those you have blessed,
>    Not of those who have earned your anger,
>    Not of those who have lost the way.

The Qur'an contains several types of verses. Some verses convey *general principles,* like urging justice and fairness. Other verses *specifically* address historical aspects of the seventh century, like slavery.

Still other verses do both: they convey a general principle, but also address a specific historical situation. The verses urging kindness to orphans are some of these. Kindness to orphans is a general principle. But the verses also address the specific historical circumstances of seventh-century Arabia, where constant warfare between tribes resulted in so many orphans that taking care of them was a concern.

The Qur'an covers many subjects and themes. One theme centers on God—the worship and nature and oneness of God. A second theme concerns individual human behavior, telling us to worship God and struggle against our own selfish impulses. A third theme concerns our behavior as members of society. A fourth theme concerns nature.

In Arabic-speaking countries, even among non-Muslims, the Qur'an has long been recognized as a compelling piece of literature. But to the Western eye, English translations of the Qur'an are difficult to understand. There are several reasons for this.

First, the Qur'an is written in fourteen-hundred-year-old Classical Arabic, which nobody speaks anymore. The words have not been changed since the Qur'an was compiled soon after Muhammad's death. Muslims were careful to preserve the original words of the Qur'an, because they didn't want God's words to become corrupted. In other words, Muslims were afraid that God's words would be changed over the years, either by accident or on purpose by someone wanting to advance a particular point of view, and so Muslims were careful to preserve the original words. The Qur'an is in an ancient language that is not easy to understand.

Because it's so old, the meanings of many Qur'anic words have changed over the centuries or have many possible meanings. For example, the Arabic word for "cut" (*qata'a*) can mean "cut," as in "to cut a piece of fruit with a knife," or it can mean "stop," as in "to cut off someone's sentence." Understanding whether it means "cut" or "stop" in a particular passage of the Qur'an might be crucial. Not all Muslims agree on what every word in the Qur'an means.

This sort of disagreement about language is something that arises in our own modern world as well. For example, even though we have preserved the exact words of the Constitution of the United States, we still debate their meanings and whether they apply to certain situations. The Qur'an is many times older than the Constitution, so it's not surprising that its meanings can be disputed.

The second reason the Qur'an is difficult to understand is that the historical and social circumstances to which the Qur'an refers have changed completely. We dress differently now, speak differently, harbor different ideas of how to behave, and think of justice in different terms. The people and culture and customs addressed by the Qur'an existed fourteen hundred years ago. That's why, before we can understand the Qur'an, we must understand Muhammad's time, with its culture and language, because that's what the Qur'an was addressing.

Historical context is especially important because some verses in the Qur'an were meant to apply only to what was happening in the seventh century. In addition, some parts of the Qur'an were responses to specific questions or issues that arose in Muhammad's community. In fact, some verses tried to *limit* historical practices.

For example, slavery existed everywhere in the world

in the seventh century and was not legally abolished until the nineteenth century—and even then there was resistance to outlawing it. If the Qur'an had tried to ban slavery over a thousand years before that, there would have been even greater resistance, because it was so acceptable everywhere in the world. In fact, banning slavery outright would have made people less likely to follow Muhammad's religion. Therefore, the Qur'an *limited* slavery with the goal of eventually phasing it out: it gave slaves certain rights, allowed slaves to buy their own freedom, and urged people to set their slaves free. Now that slavery is illegal, the Qur'anic verses on slavery are no longer relevant.

Those who do not understand this historical context could come across the mention of slavery in the Qur'an and assume that the Qur'an encourages it. This would be incorrect. The Qur'an never *advocates* slavery. The Prophet Muhammad bought slaves in order to set them free, and he urged his followers to do the same. The Bible, too, accepts slavery as a practice of the time,[2] but that does not mean that Christians accept it any longer. An understanding of history is crucial when reading ancient books.

The third reason that the Qur'an is difficult to understand relates to translation. Over 80 percent of Muslims in the world do not speak Arabic as their first language. Unless we learn Classical Arabic ourselves, we rely on translations, which cannot be as accurate as the original text. In fact, Muslims believe that a translation of the

Qur'an is not the true Qur'an. This is because language does not translate exactly, and sometimes the true meaning is lost. Anyone who has tried to translate a joke into another language realizes how difficult that is! It often just doesn't come out funny.

Arabic in particular doesn't translate easily to English. Its grammar and structure are very different. It is also a poetic and flowery language, and sometimes a single word has many layers of meaning. Here's a simple example: when someone brings you coffee, you thank him by saying, "May God bless your hands!"

The Qur'an is in verse, and poetry is especially difficult to translate. What is poetic in one language may not be poetic in another. And, like other poems, the Qur'an does not always give detailed explanations. It might *allude* to an ancient historical event, but it might not describe it in detail. Such an event might have been familiar to seventh-century people, but it may be completely bewildering to twenty-first-century readers.

The pronouns ("he," "she," "it," "they") also function differently in Arabic than in English, and this can cause confusion. Sometimes what could be translated as "he and she" is instead translated as "he." There are other instances, too, where the Qur'an actually addresses women more than it seems to do when read in an English translation.

Finally, the Qur'an must be read *intratextually*—that is, the Qur'an must be read as a whole. Too many people pick out a single phrase from the Qur'an and ignore the rest. Sometimes two or more Qur'anic verses seem to contradict one another until they are read with other verses on the same subject and in their proper historical context. To find the correct Qur'anic meaning, we must read each verse in light of other verses. Reading only one verse at random will not accurately convey what the Qur'an says on a particular subject.

You may be wondering, "If you need all this to understand the Qur'an, how do ordinary people understand it?" We must study the Qur'an's history and culture and language in order to understand it, just as we study Shakespeare's history and culture and language to understand his plays. Shakespeare's plays are difficult enough to understand without explanations of his historical context—and the Qur'an is a thousand years older than Shakespeare's plays.

Almost any text can be manipulated to justify an action. For example, some people justified American slavery on the basis of the Bible, just as some people justified slavery on the basis of the Qur'an. Some people have justified the persecution of Jews and black people on the basis of the Bible, just as some people have justified hostility toward Jews on the basis of the Qur'an. And people of numerous religious backgrounds have justified violence on the basis of religion.

But all religious texts, including the Qu'ran, must be read in historical context. In order to understand the Qur'an, we must take into account the various factors discussed in this chapter.

## The Shariah and the Sunnah

*Shariah* is an Arabic word with multiple meanings. Literally, it means "the road to the place of water." But "shariah" has a religious meaning, too, which can be translated as "the straight path" or "the path of the righteous" or "the way of God." Put another way, "shariah" means "the path of goodness that God wants me to follow."

All religions contain, in some form, the idea that people should behave in a certain way to be morally good people. The Ten Commandments is another example of a set of rules meant to guide our behavior so that we become morally good. In Islam, Muslims should follow shariah, or "the way of God," to be morally good.

But how can Muslims know what the way of God *is*? Well, nobody can know for sure, but the early Muslims looked to the Qur'an and the *Sunnah* to help them find the answer to the question, "What is the way of God?" "The Sunnah" is the name used for the words and deeds of the Prophet Muhammad. The Qur'an and the Sunnah together are the basis of Islam.

But the Qur'an and the Sunnah do not always specifically answer every question that may arise in life, such as, "Is it okay if I go to the school dance?" While Muhammad lived, the early Muslims asked him their questions. But after he died, they had to find their own answers. To do this, they began to analyze the Qur'an and the Sunnah. They tried to find general principles in the Qur'an and the Sunnah that they could use to make into new religious guidelines.

They often reached different answers to the same questions. They did not all interpret the Qur'an and the Sunnah in the same way. They frequently debated and disagreed with one another. But they accepted one another's answers as valid, because they understood that none of them could know for certain what the way of God was—they were all doing their best to understand what it could be.

Over the centuries, Islamic scholars filled thousands of books of possible answers to questions about Islam, on all kinds of subjects. These books are filled with their opinions, disagreements, and debates. Today, we refer to all these books collectively as *fiqh*, or "understanding."

Fiqh consists of the man-made religious guidelines of Islam, based on interpretations of the Qur'an and the Sunnah, written mostly in the first five hundred years of Islam. Fiqh is not a sacred text, like the Qur'an. Rather, fiqh is analysis and commentary *based on* the sacred texts.

The fiqh is not a list of rules. Rather, the fiqh contains many possible interpretations and even contradictory rules. It's a conglomeration of many different possible answers to the question "What do we do to comply with the way of God?"

Therefore, the *shariah* is the way of God, whereas the *fiqh* is the human attempt to understand the way of God. The shariah does not change, since it is the abstract, ideal

God's law. But the fiqh *can* change and was indeed *meant* to develop and change, according to the historical time and place. The rules in the classical fiqh are not set in stone. Islamic scholars today continue to interpret the religious texts and arrive at new answers to our modern questions.

The confusing thing about the word "shariah" is that it does not have a single meaning. It does mean "the road to the place of water" and "the way of God." But "shariah" can also mean the Qur'an and the Sunnah together as the sacred texts of Islam. Even more confusing, it can mean "the Qur'an *plus* the Sunnah *plus* the fiqh." Take a look at these equations—they represent the different meanings of "shariah":

Shariah = the abstract, ideal way of God
Shariah = Qur'an + Sunnah
Shariah = Qur'an + Sunnah + fiqh

The bottom equation can be especially confusing, because even though the Qur'an and Sunnah cannot change (as they are sacred texts), the fiqh *can* change. When people refer to the whole thing as "shariah," they mistakenly assume that *none* of it can change.

In addition to these meanings, shariah can also mean simply "Islam." That's because, taken together, the Qur'an and the Sunnah and the fiqh *are* Islam. It's confusing even for Muslims.

There are six core principles of shariah. These were

based on the Qur'an and developed by early Islamic scholars. These principles of shariah say that all people have

> the right to life,
> the right to family,
> the right to education,
> the right to human dignity,
> the right to religion, and
> the right to resources.

These six principles are called the *maqasid al-shariah*, which means "the objectives of the shariah." All Islamic religious guidelines must comply with these principles.

When I was growing up as a practicing Muslim, I never heard the word "shariah." Practicing Islam was about praying, fasting, honesty, charity, belief in God and Muhammad, Eid, modesty, and not much beyond that. I never thought in terms of shariah—it was just Islam I was practicing.

Sometimes Qur'an and Sunnah and fiqh together are all referred to as "Islamic law." Sometimes shariah is also called "Islamic law." I myself have a degree in "Islamic law"! But "Islamic law" is a misleading term, because it implies that shariah is "law" like our state or federal laws, which are made and enforced by the government. It is not. Shariah (or Islamic law) is actually a set of religious guidelines and a personal code of religious conduct.

Shariah is not the law of the land anywhere in the

world; that is, no country is governed by "shariah." Muslim-majority countries have their own laws and constitutions. Muslims, wherever they are in the world, must comply with their country's laws first and foremost.

As an American Muslim, I see no conflict between the laws of the United States and Islam. I am free to practice my religion, just as others are free to practice theirs. In fact, being Muslim requires me to comply with the laws of my country, because in Islam citizenship is a *trust* (like a contract or a promise), which cannot be broken.

Islam is continually developing and changing. No religion survives for fourteen hundred years and becomes the second-largest in the world without being flexible and adaptable. And although Muslims cannot change the Qur'an, we can change our *understanding* of the Qur'an. Muslim scholars all over the world today are continuing to develop the fiqh for our modern world, in a variety of ways, both traditional and nontraditional.

## Chapter 14

# From Sand Dunes to Spain:
# The Spread of Islam

By the time Muhammad died, his followers numbered in the tens of thousands. That sounds like a lot. But it was not enough to fill a modern football stadium!

After Muhammad's death, chaos erupted. Certain tribes that had joined Muhammad broke their peace treaties with the Muslims. They assumed that since Muhammad was dead, their peace treaties were canceled and they could fight the Muslims.

This is not surprising, because that was their culture. The Muslims had a new religion, but their Arabian culture was the only culture they knew, and it was deeply ingrained in them. They fought the rebelling tribes and secured their borders. But then, elated by their success, they simply kept fighting, and their borders began to expand.

Muhammad had never instigated warfare or engaged in war that was not in self-defense. But his successors did. The Arabs were a relatively small number of people. Yet they dismantled two enormous empires—the Roman-Byzantine empire and the Persian empire. How did they do it with so few people and resources?

First, the Roman-Byzantine empire and the Persian empire had been fighting each other for a long time. Fighting each other was hard enough, but suddenly they had to contend with a new (Arab) army attacking them. This gave the Arabs an advantage.

Second, the local people in the Roman-Byzantine and Persian empires were tired of fighting, and consequently they often helped the Arabs. Jews and non-Orthodox Christians, who were frequently persecuted by their rulers in some areas, viewed the Arabs as liberators. For example, Egyptian Coptic Christians turned Egypt over to the Arabs in 640; Jews in Palestine and Syria helped the Arabs because they were tired of Roman persecution.[1]

Third, sometimes the Arabs did not bother to attack, but simply sent the rulers a proposal to surrender. If the rulers accepted the proposal, they relinquished power to the Arabs. But why would they do this?

In some cases, they did not think they could win. Their resources might have been depleted in previous wars. They might have been tired of fighting. Whatever the reason, some rulers did choose to surrender.

The purpose of the seventh- and eighth-century Arab conquests was to gain territory and govern it, not spread religion. In fact, during this time, the Arabs did not particularly *want* people to convert to Islam; they liked to think of themselves as an elite, chosen people. For the most part, the Arabs were content to let local populations keep their religion and culture, pay a tax in return, and leave ruling to the Arabs. In other words, the Arabs conquered territory not to forcibly convert people to Islam but to increase their *political rule.*

The Western stereotype has traditionally portrayed Islam as a religion that Muslims spread by forcing people to convert or die. In fourteen hundred years of Islamic history, it's inevitable that there would be some incidents of forced conversion. But these were relatively rare, and the historical record shows that the spread of Islam was not characterized by a policy of forced conversion. In fact, during the first two centuries of Islamic rule, local populations remained mostly non-Muslim.

I remember my high school history teacher telling my class, "The Qur'an says that Islam is supposed to be spread by the sword." This is not true. The Qur'an contains many statements *prohibiting* forced conversion, such as: "There is no compulsion in religion"[2] and "To you your religion, to me mine!"[3] and "If God had desired it, everyone on earth would have believed; are you then going to compel the people to become believers?"[4]

Historically, Jews, Christians, Zoroastrians, Hindus, and other groups under Islamic rule kept their religious and cultural laws and in return paid a tax called the *jizya*. This tax also exempted them from military duty. These groups also did not have to pay the zakat tax to the government, which Muslims paid. Likewise, Muslims didn't pay the jizya tax.

The jizya tax was not always imposed on non-Muslims. Usually women, the elderly, the poor, and religious clerics were exempt from the tax. (Historically, poor non-Muslims were also entitled to money from the government's zakat fund.) And from time to time Muslim rulers waived the jizya as a goodwill gesture for certain people or populations.[5]

Because people were taxed differently, depending on their religion, this was not equal citizenship the way we think of it now. But laws in ancient times were typically based on religious affiliation. Even many centuries later, taxes based on religion were common; as late as the nineteenth century in England, Catholics paid a tax in exchange for not joining the Anglican Church. In the seventh and eight centuries, leaving non-Muslims alone to practice their own religion and culture in return for a tax showed a tolerant attitude. In fact, Jews and Christians within the Islamic empire were able to advance to high positions as scholars, finance ministers, and governors.

The jizya and taxes like it are historical practices that are no longer relevant. It is no longer considered just or fair to treat people differently on the basis of religion. According to the modern Muslim view, the Qur'an allowed the jizya tax as a solution for a particular historical situation that no longer exists. Therefore, the jizya is no longer applicable.

After the Arab conquests of the seventh and eighth centuries, many people who lived under Muslim rule did eventually convert to Islam. Sometimes they converted because they believed in the religious message of Islam. But they converted for other reasons as well. Some married Muslims. Some did better under Islam than under their own clan or class structure. Some didn't want to pay the jizya tax anymore. Some identified with the new Arab culture, and some wanted to be part of the ruling class.

The Arab conquests, like other conquests at that time, were wars to gain territory and power. But in waging war the Arabs ran into a problem: the Qur'an allows warfare only in self-defense, and wars for territory are not self-defense. So how did the early Muslims get around this restriction?

The early Muslims lived at a time in which invasion and conquest was taken for granted. They had to conquer or be conquered. They couldn't conceive of any other way of surviving. So they simply ignored the verses that prevented them from waging war. They tried to reconcile their new religion (which prohibited wars for territory) with their old cultural practices (which allowed wars for territory). Their old cultural practices won.

In addition to conquest, the religion of Islam spread

by trade and by migration. The Arabs sailed to Southeast Asia to trade, and some settled there. Traders and Sufi migrations in the early centuries of Islam contributed largely to the spread of Islam in India.

By 750 CE, the Islamic empire—by then not only Arab, but a mix of ethnicities—had grown so large that it straddled three continents, stretching across four-thousand miles. At that point, the Muslims mostly ceased expanding their empire and settled down to govern it. They began to nurture scholarship with such zeal that Islamic civilization became one of the most advanced on earth and remained so for nearly a thousand years.

Every Muslim has an obligation to seek knowledge. This is called *'ilm*. I was told, growing up, that it was even more important for women to seek knowledge than for men, because women were often in better positions to pass knowledge on to their children.

As the early Muslims conquered various territories and came into contact with other cultures, they began to acquire knowledge voraciously. Baghdad, seat of the Islamic empire, became the scholarly center of the civilized world. If the Arabs had not gathered knowledge, recorded it, and translated it, the works of ancient Greeks such as Pythagoras and Aristotle might never have survived. Islamic civilization flowered intellectually, not only preserving ancient scholarship but also correcting it, challenging it, and making new discoveries.

Islamic civilization's contributions to the world of science were so significant that we still use Arabic terms like "algorithm," "chemist," "cipher," "zenith," "zero," and "algebra" in our modern scientific language.

The Arabs recognized the practicality of the Indian numerical system and put it into widespread use; we still use Arabic numerals today. The concept of *zero* (*sifr* in Arabic) was brought to medieval Europe by the Arabs. Zero was a difficult concept for many premodern cultures, and it confused the Europeans. They pronounced the Arabic word *sifr* as "cipher." This confusion resulted in a common saying: "Oh, he's saying something totally incomprehensible, like a cipher"—that is, "like a zero." From there, the English word "cipher" came to mean an incomprehensible message—namely, a coded message.[6]

Arab Muslims invented *cryptanalysis,* the science of code breaking, or unscrambling secret messages. Before the Arabs, no one had devised a method for breaking codes. A civilization had to achieve a high level of linguistics, mathematics, and statistics before that was possible.[7]

The first known available treatise on cryptanalysis was written by the Arab philosopher al-Kindi in the ninth century. This book was discovered only in 1987, in an archive in Istanbul. It refers to another Arab treatise on the subject dated even earlier, from the eighth century, but that manuscript has not been found.

The pursuit of knowledge resulted in the establishment of libraries, bookshops, and centers of translation and research. In the early 800s, the ruling caliph established in Baghdad the research institute known as the

Bayt al-Hikmah. He invited all the best scholars there, whether they were Muslim or not.

The Muslims gathered texts in Chinese, Armenian, Hebrew, Greek, Latin, Persian, Coptic, Syriac, and Sanskrit and translated them into Arabic. In fact, the Muslims placed so much value on acquiring knowledge that, despite their military superiority, they offered a peace treaty to the Romans in exchange for all their Greek manuscripts.

The Arabs had centers for copying and preserving texts—they had learned the art of making paper from the Chinese—and published tens of thousands of books a year. (This was before the printing press.) At a time when books were rare and precious in other parts of the world, streets in Baghdad were lined with hundreds of bookshops.

Among the subjects studied in the ninth-century Islamic empire were philosophy, astronomy, mathematics, linguistics, physics, chemistry, and medicine. An Arab mathematician named al-Khwarizmi developed a new field of mathematics, which he called *al-jabr* and which, by the time it reached Europe, came to be known as algebra. The word "algorithm" comes from a mispronunciation of al-Khwarizmi's name.

It was Muslim physicians who first realized that blood circulated throughout the body; their medical texts were used for hundreds of years, as far away as Europe. They explained how vision worked, developed the science of optics, and were able to remove cataracts (when the lens in the eye becomes cloudy and hard to see through).[8] Eleventh-century Muslim scholar Ibn Sina wrote more than 276 scholarly books on various subjects; his text on medicine was translated eighty-seven times and was the basis of European medical teaching and practice for four hundred years.

Muslim artists fashioned ceramics, paintings, and some of the most intricate textiles in history. The words "alkali," "saffron," "taffeta," "damask," and "organdy" come from Arabic. Because Islamic textiles were prized above any others in the world, they often shrouded the bones of Christian saints.

Mathematicians are only now realizing that some mathematical results had been proved centuries before Western scholarship discovered them. The first writings in statistics appeared in Arabic over a thousand years ago. The Arabs used combinatorics (the science of mathematical arrangements) some twelve hundred years ago.[9]

Why are we only now realizing the extent of Islamic scholarship? Manuscripts and documents did not always survive through the centuries. Sometimes manuscripts were archived on some dusty shelf in an ancient vault or made inaccessible by political problems or warfare. Documents deteriorated or were accidentally destroyed. Some were purposely destroyed by invaders. And differences in language and culture meant that those outside Islamic civilization sometimes simply did not understand the extent of Islamic scholarship.

The great Islamic civilizations were ruled by different

peoples and different dynasties, peaking at different times in history. The Islamic empire had its seat in Baghdad; the Ottoman empire had its seat in Istanbul; parts of Spain were ruled by Muslims for eight hundred years; and the Mughal empire in India had its seat in Delhi. These civilizations had all declined by the nineteenth century (and some well before that). By the early twentieth century, most Muslim lands had been conquered or colonized by Western powers. Many of the modern Muslim-majority countries in the world today, like Algeria, received their independence in the mid-twentieth century; some, like Iraq and Jordan, were not created until the twentieth century.

## Jihad and Violence in the Name of Islam

*Jihad* is one of the most misunderstood Islamic concepts. In the news, the word is sometimes defined as "holy war." But Islamic law has no concept of "holy war." In Islam, war is never holy; rather, it is either justified or unjustified.[10] Sometimes, the terms "jihad" and "terrorism" are incorrectly used interchangeably, and terrorists are called "jihadists." In actuality, the complete opposite is true—terrorism has always been a violation of Islamic law. Terrorists can never be exercising jihad, because terrorism violates Islam.

"Jihad" means "effort" or "struggle." This can be an internal struggle or an external struggle. The internal jihad is a struggle to improve oneself. The external jihad is to correct injustice in society.

This *internal* jihad to improve oneself is called "jihad by the heart." Muslims might wage a jihad by the heart for education or to cultivate patience or to eliminate selfishness. The internal jihad is about the individual.

The *external* jihad is about society. It is the struggle to eliminate injustice or oppression. This external jihad may take several forms.

First, Muslims may undertake "jihad by the tongue." This means using speech and verbal persuasion to correct an injustice. An example of jihad by the tongue would be writing letters to editors of newspapers and publishing essays on the Internet.

Second, Muslims may undertake jihad by the hands. This means doing good works to overthrow oppression. For example, feeding the homeless is a type of jihad by the hands.

Finally, if nothing else works, Muslims may undertake "jihad by the sword," which is the use of force in self-defense or to overthrow oppression. Some Islamic scholars say that, before force may be used, the oppression must actually prevent Muslims from practicing their religion. Jihad by the sword is never war for territory, war to convert people to Islam, war to get revenge, or war because you feel like it. It is only warfare in self-defense or to overthrow oppression.

This doesn't mean that Muslims have never waged war. The Arab conquests, for example, were not wars in self-defense, but political wars waged in accordance with seventh-century culture. Some (but not all) early Muslim scholars advocated theories that would allow them to wage war to spread Islamic political rule, but that attitude became obsolete relatively early in Islamic history.

Christianity and Islam had similar rules of war in ancient times. Both accepted wars for religion or wars justified by religion. But they both eventually rejected that idea. For centuries, Islamic law has allowed warfare only in self-defense or to overthrow oppression.

Jihad by the sword can be declared only by a recognized and accepted leader of all Muslims. There is no such leader in the world today. Even if there were, jihad by the sword is restricted by numerous stringent rules, some of which are the following:

- the war must be in self-defense or to overthrow oppression;
- the "oppression" you're trying to overthrow must be a direct oppression (like someone not letting you practice your religion or get food);
- the self-defense must be immediate and not something that happened in the past;
- you cannot use secret force (like sneaking into enemy camp and planting bombs);
- you cannot use treachery (like pretending to be on someone's side but secretly acting against that person);
- you can kill only people who are fighting in the war;

- you may not kill people who are not fighting in the war, even if they're associated with the enemy (such as the soldiers' families);
- you cannot arbitrarily destroy property;
- you cannot wage war against fellow Muslims;
- you cannot cheat (for example, you cannot sign a peace treaty with the intention of breaking it and tricking the enemy);
- you cannot kill people who take refuge in holy buildings;
- you cannot kill children, the elderly, "men of the cloth" (monks, rabbis, priests), or other noncombatants;
- you cannot commit acts of terrorism (defined as the secret use of force); and
- you cannot commit suicide.

When Muslim criminals attacked the World Trade Center on September 11, 2001, they committed an egregious crime under Islamic law. The attacks were not jihad. The attackers violated numerous rules of Islam by engaging in terrorism, murdering civilians, committing suicide, destroying property, killing people not fighting in a war, and acting not in self-defense or to overthrow a direct oppression but for other reasons.

Tens of thousands of statements by Muslim leaders and organizations and individuals condemned the September 11 attacks as criminal acts. Leaders of numerous Muslim-majority countries sent messages of sympathy to the United States government. Muslims, like people of all religions, commit crimes. That doesn't mean Islam allows them to do so.

When Muhammad and his followers resided in Mecca, their jihad took the form of nonviolent resistance. Muhammad is reported to have said, "The best form of jihad is to speak the truth in the face of an oppressive ruler." He led his followers in these acts of nonviolent resistance:

- first secret and then public preaching of their faith;
- keeping their faith, despite persecution;
- freeing slaves who had converted to Islam;
- emigration to Abyssinia (now Ethiopia); and
- emigration to Medina.[11]

It was only when hostilities continued after they moved to Medina that Muhammad gave the Muslims permission to fight back in self-defense.[12] Whenever a Qur'anic verse allows warfare, it limits that warfare with another verse, such as "But do not attack them unless they attack you first"[13] and "God loves not the aggressor"[14] and "If they incline to peace, you must incline to peace"[15] and:

> *Thus, if they let you be*
> *And do not make war on you*

> *And offer you peace,*
> *God does not allow you to harm them.*[16]

These verses forbid Muslims from attacking first. That is why the vast majority of Muslims today consider jihad to be defensive warfare.

The Qur'anic verses that urge fighting apply only to Muhammad's particular historical situation and to the conflict that was going on at the time. These verses gave permission to fight only with the Meccans and with particular people who had broken the peace treaty with the Muslims. The Qur'an was not urging Muslims to go *start* a fight; it allowed them to fight back when they were attacked in an *ongoing* conflict.

Some Muslim extremists isolate the "fighting" verses and ignore both the "peace" verses and the historical context, all so that they can justify warfare. Some non-Muslims do the same, to prove that Muslims are violent. But that's not an accurate portrayal of Islamic law.

Throughout history, religions have been used to justify warfare and even criminal behavior. This does not mean that the religions themselves are violent or that everyone who follows them is violent. Of the 6,236 or so verses of the Qur'an, fewer than 1 percent relate to warfare. They must be read alongside the many more verses that urge peace.

# Part III

# Modern Muslim Demographics

# Chapter 15

# Who's Who: Sunni, Shi'a, Sufi, and More

I have a Muslim acquaintance who reached adulthood before it occurred to her to ask her father, "Are we Sunni or Shi'a?"

Her father replied, "We are *Muslim*."

As a child, I never paid attention to whether our Muslim friends were Sunni or Shi'a. We all attended the same mosques. We socialized together and prayed together.

This was not just an American phenomenon. My father attended a mosque in India that was attended by both Sunni and Shi'a. Mosques all over the world have mixed congregations of Sunni and Shi'a. Intermarriages between Sunni and Shi'i Muslims are so common as to be unremarkable.

The difference between Sunni and Shi'a goes back to the time of Muhammad's death, when his followers had to choose a new leader for their community. Muhammad had been both the prophet and the community leader for the Muslims. No one could replace him as a prophet, but the Muslims did need a leader.

They debated how to choose their next leader. One group of Muslims believed leadership should remain in Muhammad's family. Ali, the Prophet's cousin and son-in-law (he had married Muhammad's daughter Fatima), was their candidate. The Muslims who nominated Ali eventually came to be called the *Shi'at-Ali*, or "the Party of Ali." This was shortened to *Shi'a*.

Another group, however, believed that the new leader should be selected by *consensus* or election. They wanted to distance themselves from the traditional clan system of leadership, in which leadership stayed within a particular family. This group eventually came to be called the *Sunni*, or "those who follow the Sunnah."

The second group prevailed, and Abu Bakr, the Prophet Muhammad's friend and father-in-law, became the caliph. A caliph was not a prophet or religious leader but a social and political leader, like a governor. Abu Bakr and the three caliphs who governed after him—Umar, Uthman, and Ali—were all companions of the Prophet. After Ali, however, rulers disregarded the system of consensus, and leadership in the Islamic empire became *dynastic* (passed down from father to son).

In Sunni Islam, religious scholars are considered the

*religious authorities.* Traditionally, Muslims look to them to make the rules and answer the questions about Islam. Even then, however, religious scholars do not have *binding* authority—that is, a Muslim can choose to follow or not follow a particular scholar.

For the Shi'a, religious authority is more complicated. The Shi'a believe that religious authority passed from the Prophet to his male descendants. Most Shi'a (those known as "Twelvers") recognize twelve male descendants of Prophet Muhammad. These descendants are called *Imams.* The Shi'a consider these descendants to have been divinely guided, though not prophets themselves. (These Imams are different from "imams" who simply lead prayers or are simply scholars of Islam.) The line of Imams died out when the twelfth Imam disappeared. He will return, it is said, in the time of his community's greatest need.

Aside from the Twelvers, there are several minority groups of Shi'i. The *Zaydis* and *Ismailis* are two of them. The Zaydis recognize Muhammad's descendants as Imams, but not divinely guided ones. The Ismailis believe that the Prophet Muhammad's line of descendants never died out and that their leader, called the *Aga Khan,* is a direct descendant of the Prophet; in Ismaili Islam, the Aga Khan is the religious authority.

Today, 85 to 90 percent of the Muslims in the world are Sunni and 10 to 15 percent are Shi'a. The Sunni have four main schools of religious law, and the Shi'a have one main school of religious law, but they all recognize each other as valid. Neither Sunni nor Shi'a are "orthodox," and neither broke off from the other. They developed side by side.

When the line of Shi'i Imams died out, religious leadership passed from them to the Shi'i religious scholars. Since then, in both Shi'i and Sunni traditions, the religious scholars have made the religious rules (the Ismailis being the exception, because the Aga Khan is the religious authority). Today, in practice, Sunni and Shi'a are not very different from one another, aside from small differences in rituals and the commemoration of Ashura.

## The Sufis

Sufism is the aspect of Islam that has become most popular throughout the Western world. The Sufis are not a separate group of Muslims. Sufism is a *spiritual way* of practicing Islam, and Sufis can be Shi'a or Sunni.

Imagine a circle that represents the guidelines of Islam. Imagine the center point of the circle, which represents God. From anywhere on the circle, you can draw a line to the center point. That line is the Sufi Way. It works like this: once you're a Muslim and you stand on the circle of Islam, you can follow the Sufi Way (the line) to the center point, which represents God.

The Sufi movement began over a thousand years ago, because a group of Muslims were disgusted by the materialism they saw in society. They felt that people cared too much about what they owned and what they wanted to

own. They believed that other Muslims were overly concerned with the rules and regulations of Islam and were
missing the point of the Prophet Muhammad's message.
This group of Muslims based their beliefs on the Prophet,
who was a frugal and humble person, and on the messages of the Qur'an that emphasize God's beauty, compassion, mercy, and benevolence—asserting, correctly,
that there are many more of these verses than of those
emphasizing God's wrath and punishment. Giving up
their possessions, they donned a coarse woollen garment
as part of their practice of shunning wealth. They came to
be called *Sufi*—a word that means "wool."

Sufis emphasize introspection (the examination of
one's own mind and feelings) and achieving nearness to
God. Different Sufi groups use different methods for this
purpose. Some Sufis use chanting to attain a state of
meditation, in order to bring them nearer to God. Some
Sufis use music and dancing.

You may have come across photographs of *whirling
dervishes*. In Istanbul, I watched Sufi men dressed in
full-skirted white tunics and trousers whirling to music.
Whirling helps them achieve a state of meditation and
oneness with God. It is an art form that is beautiful to
watch.

## The Nation of Islam

The Nation of Islam is a group that originated in
the United States, independent of mainstream Islam.

Originally, many of its tenets differed significantly from even the basic beliefs of mainstream Islam. Whether the Nation of Islam should be considered part of Islam at all is currently in dispute.

The Nation of Islam began in the early twentieth century as an African American nationalist movement. Just a few decades before that, in 1865, the Thirteenth Amendment to the U.S. Constitution had abolished slavery. That meant that many African Americans in the early twentieth century were former slaves or the children of former slaves.

More than that, many African Americans were descendants of *Muslim* slaves. According to some estimates, around 20 percent of the slaves brought to the United States from Africa were Muslim. They did not remain Muslim for long, though, as keeping their religion in a slave environment was very difficult.

In the early twentieth century, only a few generations after the end of slavery, discrimination and prejudice against African Americans was still rampant. African Americans needed positive ways to think about their own identity and to form their own support groups. The Nation of Islam helped them fulfill both those needs.

Timothy Drew founded the Nation of Islam in 1913. He and his successors developed a new religion that contained some elements of Islam and some of Christianity, but was separate and different from both. He called it the Nation of Islam to distance it from Christianity, the primary religion among white Americans; he may also have wanted to reclaim a lost Islamic heritage. But the name has always caused confusion, especially as members of the Nation of Islam were sometimes called Black Muslims.

The Nation of Islam was a social movement as well as a religious movement, stressing ways to help African Americans with their lives. Drew's goal was to free his people from prejudice and discrimination. Despite those goals, the Nation of Islam was heavily criticized by white Americans, because its leaders sometimes preached offensive, racist messages and also because it was a *separatist* movement—that is, its leaders advocated forming a separate country without white people, since they did not receive full citizenship privileges in the United States at that time. But the movement also helped African Americans take pride in their identity, fight crime in the inner cities, and promote healthy habits and discipline.

In 1964, something began to change in the Nation of Islam. One of its ministers, Malcolm X, traveled to Mecca for the Hajj. Malcolm X was a gifted and popular speaker, but he had angered white Americans with his inflammatory and, at times, racist remarks. When he made his pilgrimage to Mecca, he realized how totally different Islam was from the "Nation of Islam." Coming to Mecca as part of a separatist movement based on race, he was amazed by how many different races and nationalities were represented at the Hajj. His wife, Betty Shabazz, observed that Malcolm went to Mecca as a Black Muslim and came back as a Muslim.[1] He brought his newfound enthusiasm for Islam back to the Nation of Islam. He was assassinated in 1965, but his ideas influenced W. D. Muhammad, who became the leader of the Nation of Islam in 1975.

W. D. Muhammad began working to change the beliefs and practices of the Nation of Islam to become more aligned with Sunni Islam. The name of the organization was changed to The World Community of al-Islam in the West. In 1980, the name was again changed to the American Muslim Mission. By this time, the organization had completed the transformation to Sunni Islam.

But a small group of Nation of Islam members resisted the change. They broke off from the main group and kept the original name and philosophy of the Nation of Islam. This group, currently led by Louis Farrakhan, is still called the Nation of Islam. Most African American Muslims in the United States today are Sunni Muslims.

## Wahhabis and Taliban

In the eighteenth century, over a thousand years after Islam was born, a man named Abd al-Wahhab began preaching on the Arabian peninsula in the area that would one day become Saudi Arabia. Abd al-Wahhab preached his own version of Islam—a new, rigid, intolerant form that combined religion with the conservative, patriarchal culture of the Arabian peninsula.

Abd al-Wahhab and his followers (called *Wahhabis*) were denounced as extremists by many Islamic scholars of the time. His movement might have fizzled away eventually, as most extremist groups do, but something inter-vened. The Wahhabi movement found a partner.

The al-Saud family wanted to rule the Arabian penin-sula, and they needed allies. They agreed to adopt Abd al-Wahhab's religion if he and his followers supported them. He did, and when the al-Saud family eventually did take over the area and establish Saudi Arabia in 1932, Wahhabi Islam became the official religion of the country.

Wahhabi Islam is still the official religion of Saudi Arabia, though not all Saudis are Wahhabi. Although Wahhabism has relaxed somewhat since the eighteenth century, it is still an extreme version of Islam, and it is still very intermingled with the culture of the Arabian penin-sula. And although the different schools of Islamic law have always accepted each other as equally valid, Wahhabism does not accept the others as valid.

Fewer than 2 percent of Muslims worldwide are Wah-habi. Nevertheless, they have been disproportionately in-fluential because Saudi Arabia is an oil-rich country, is in charge of the two Muslim holy cities of Mecca and Me-dina, and has powerful Western countries as allies. But Saudis have also been disproportionately influential be-cause Western media often portray them as representa-tive of all Muslims, using terms like "Islam Central" and "the purest form of Islam," terms with which most Mus-lims worldwide would not agree.

The Taliban are limited to certain parts of Afghanistan

and Pakistan and constitute a fraction of 1 percent of Muslims worldwide. They are militarized Wahhabis. They were trained in Wahhabi schools and armed during Afghanistan's war with the Soviets in the 1980s. After the war, Afghanistan was left in chaos. The Taliban, a group of armed Afghans, rose to power, promising to restore order.

At first they were welcomed, because Afghan society was in disarray. However, the Taliban became so brutal and extreme that today they are not recognized by any Muslim country as legitimate. They take the law into their own hands and intimidate and brutalize people at will; in this sense, they are no different from any other group of people who use violence to get power for themselves. Although they portray themselves as religious, they violate Islamic law by committing murder and many other crimes.

The Taliban are not just anti-American. They are opposed to *anyone* who challenges their authority, including other Muslims. They have destroyed Shi'i artifacts in Afghanistan, as well as Buddhist artifacts.

*Chapter 16*

## Muslims: Who We Are
## and Where We Live

Recently I attended a conference in Malaysia to promote women's rights from an Islamic point of view. Our goal was to use Islam and the shariah (including the six principles of shariah discussed in Chapter 13) to argue for equal rights for women.

Over two hundred Muslim women from forty-five countries, as well as some men, attended the conference. The women wore all sorts of clothing. About three-quarters of them did not cover their hair, but some did. Not one covered her face. The women wore pants, chadors, robes, dresses, long skirts, short skirts, long sleeves, short sleeves, and no sleeves.

The conference reminded me how varied Muslims

are, in their way of life and in their dress. We're all affected, like everyone, by hundreds of factors, such as wealth, poverty, family life, schooling, friends, warfare, siblings, the state of our health, hunger, language, and access to medical care and education. This chapter is intended to open a small window onto the Muslim population in the world—where we live, some of the ways in which we view the world, and some of the challenges we face.

## Muslims Worldwide

Approximately 1.5 billion Muslims live in the world. This amounts to between one-fifth and one-fourth of the world's total population. Islam is the second-largest religion in the world.

Only 12 to 20 percent of the world's Muslims are Arab. Estimates vary because people don't usually have to report their religion and because it's hard to define "Arab." We could define "Arab" as someone who speaks Arabic, but many non-Arab people learn or speak Arabic. We could define "Arab" as someone from ancient "Arabia," but native Arabs from centuries ago have, by now, intermixed with other ethnic groups. For example, Moroccans speak Arabic in their country, and Arabs did settle in Morocco, but the Moroccans do not necessarily consider themselves Arab; they're Moroccan.

It may come as a surprise that Indonesia, India, Pakistan, and Bangladesh have the largest Muslim populations in the world. Together, they are home to nearly half the world's Muslims. The majority of Muslims in the world are Asian. Some fifty-seven countries have Muslim-majority populations or substantial Muslim populations.

Because these countries vary culturally and ethnically, the practice of Islam varies from country to country, too. Culture, custom, and tradition are all significant factors in how people practice their religions. Culture in Canada, for example, is vastly different from culture in Saudi Arabia, so the practice of Islam is different, too. Even Muslims within the same country practice Islam in a variety of ways, just like Christians in the United States practice Christianity in a variety of ways.

A cultural characteristic that many Muslim communities do have in common is the love of poetry. As mentioned earlier, in seventh-century Arabia, a truce was called once a year, at the time of the annual poetry festival. That love of poetry still permeates Muslim cultures. Perhaps it is because the Qur'an has a rhythm and poetry of its own. Whatever the reason, poetry in Muslim cultures is appreciated not just by intellectuals, but by everyone.

In Pakistan, an annual Urdu *mushaira* (public poetry reading) draws fifteen thousand men, women, and children every year. Pakistanis bring picnics and autograph books and sit all night on carpets spread in an outdoor arena twinkling with lights. They listen to male and female poets recite their verses, sipping *chai* (spiced tea) from the snack stands and shouting with enthusiasm when the poetry overcomes them. Millions more watch the event on television. Smaller mushairas crop up all over Pakistan throughout the year.[1]

In Somalia, where people are often so poor that a family can load all its possessions on the back of a camel, stories in verse are passed down from generation to generation. Somalis hold poetry competitions, sometimes lasting for *weeks*, outdoors under the trees. Poets are held in respect and accorded prestige.[2]

In Morocco, the ancient public square in the city of Marrakesh is called Djemaa el-Fnaa, or "Gathering of the Dead." On a sunny weekend, a poet-storyteller might trek down from the hills and settle on his carpet, amid the water sellers and python charmers, to tell his tale. He might toss his bird into the air to bring back a story and then wait until the crowd around him quiets down before he begins painting his tale in words.

Even in the United States, Muslim poetry has made an impact. Jalal al-Din Rumi, a Muslim who was born in Afghanistan and lived in Turkey in the thirteenth century, wrote such beautiful poetry in Farsi, the language of Iran, that today, over eight centuries later, he is the best-selling poet in the United States. Modern poet Mohja Kahf is an American Muslim woman whose book of poetry is called *E-mails from Scheherazad*. And Daniel Abdal-Hayy Moore's award-winning poetry springs from both the Sufi tradition and the twentieth-century American poetic tradition.

Poetry is not what we usually hear about in news reports, though. Those watching the news might receive the erroneous impression that Muslim-majority countries have nothing but problems. This is because the news media focus on the bizarre, violent, and horrific and not on the positive. However, it is true that many Muslim-majority countries are dealing with political problems and issues of injustice. These problems arise from several factors.

First, most Muslim-majority countries are part of the developing world. That means that these countries are dealing with all the problems typical of the developing world. Such problems include hunger, poverty, illiteracy, discrimination against women, religious discrimination, oppressive governments, lack of democracy, and violence. Problems like these plague all developing countries, whether they have Muslim majorities or not.

In Pakistan, for example, most people do not have access to education or good health care. Over half of Pakistanis are illiterate. Pakistanis living in the cities have access to education and resources, but those in the mountains and rural areas do not. It is hard even to get teachers to go there to teach.

In addition, the government of Pakistan has little influence over the mountain areas, so laws are difficult to enforce. The government itself has been accused of corruption for decades. Many Pakistanis do not have computers, Internet access, television, teachers, sufficient food, or clean water. All these factors affect the way people understand the world and their own communities.

Many Muslim-majority countries today wrestle with problems similar to those of Pakistan. However, Islam is not the reason for these problems, any more than Christianity is the reason for the same kinds of problems in parts of Latin America. Asian countries that are not predominantly Muslim, such as Nepal, India, and China, all wrestle with the same types of problems. So do many African countries, whatever their majority religion. They are all part of the developing world.

A second factor that has held back some Muslim populations is culture and tradition. Many Muslim-majority countries have patriarchal cultures—that is, male-dominated cultures that disadvantage women. When people confuse culture with religion, they become reluctant to change their culture. If the culture is discriminatory or premodern, this can cause problems.

The effects of patriarchal, traditional culture can be seen all over the world, in both Muslim and non-Muslim countries. In Afghanistan, where only 28 percent of the population can read and write, Muslim women are abused and even killed because they are primarily subject to their ancient tribal laws. In India, thousands of Hindu women are killed by their husbands every year for their dowries (their bridal money). In China, couples are allowed only one child; because many would prefer a boy to a girl, millions of girls have gone "missing" over the decades. In Latin American Christian-majority countries, men who have murdered their female relatives have traditionally been treated very leniently.[3] In Saudi Arabia, the conservative culture of the Arabian peninsula is at least as influential as Islam, and it results in laws that discriminate against women. In Nepal, where the population is primarily Hindu and Buddhist, thousands of women are sold into domestic slavery every year. These modern-day injustices are not the result of religion, but of culture and greed and many other factors.

A third reason Muslim countries are in turmoil is their history of *colonization*. Much of the Muslim world was colonized, or ruled by foreign powers, until the twentieth century. Western colonial powers divided Muslim lands among themselves, drawing new borders that created new countries for them to govern. The new borders often split up ethnic and religious communities, creating language difficulties and other problems.

Colonization disrupts the ability of countries to modernize. It depletes the resources of the colonized lands. It fractures national identity between the colonizers and the colonized. Sometimes, when the colonizers leave, dictators grab power; this prevents people from establishing real democracies.

It takes time for countries to get back on their feet after they gain independence from their colonizers. Muslim-majority countries have been independent for only a short time. They have some distance to go, but they are steadily improving. Since the 1990s, twenty-three Muslim-majority countries have become more democratic.[4] In the spring of 2011, peaceful protests of hundreds of thousands of Muslims all over the Middle East and North Africa toppled dictatorial regimes or brought about democratic reforms. Whatever the outcome of each particular struggle, the overall direction has been toward greater democracy.

## American Muslims

American Muslims are lucky to live in a democracy already. What are American Muslims like? Recent surveys can give us some clues. First of all, only a minority attend mosques.[5] Of those who do, women are just as likely to attend as men.[6] This is different from some Muslim-majority countries, where men are more likely to attend than women. When my father was growing up in India, he said it was the custom for women to not attend the mosque. Islam itself does not prevent women from attending the mosque; women have been praying at the Ka'ba since the beginning of Islam.

In my experience, culture is often more influential than religion. Although I am just as devout a Muslim as women in the Middle East or Asia, my lifestyle is not similar to theirs. My lifestyle is much closer to that of my American *non-Muslim* peers. I am not unusual in this respect—according to a recent poll, American Muslims are "moderate, mainstream, and middle class."[7]

Along with other American Muslim women, I do not feel that being a Muslim woman limits my opportunities. American Muslim women are one of the most highly educated female religious groups in the United States, second only to Jewish American women.[8] In the American Muslim community, men's incomes and women's incomes are more equal than those in any other religious group.[9]

The Gallup Center has found that American Muslims are the most racially diverse religious group in the

United States.[10] We are 35 percent African American, 18 percent Asian, 28 percent white, and 18 percent other. I am proud of this diversity, but it does present some challenges—it means that American Muslims must overcome language barriers and cultural differences in their own communities.

## Muslim Women in Particular

The cultural oppression of some Muslim women in the modern-day world is a tragedy, because the Qur'an clearly intended to improve women's rights. The Qur'an and Muhammad gave women more rights in seventh-century Arabia than women in other cultures had or would have for hundreds of years—more rights than, for example, Englishwomen would have for more than another *thousand* years.

Sometimes we forget that equal rights for women is a fairly new concept. American women received the right to vote only in 1920, and Swiss women received equal rights to vote in 1971. Imagine what things were like in 610, when Muhammad began preaching.

Islam was radically feminist for its time and place. In his last sermon, for example, Muhammad made several statements that were revolutionary for their time, including "O People, it is true that you have some rights with regard to your women, but they also have rights over you." For the year 632, this was a huge statement.

But because feminism was such a difficult concept for men fourteen hundred years ago, men tried to limit

women's rights, even the rights given to women in the
Qur'an. That's why the traditional Islamic fiqh (the
man-made religious rules) is not as feminist as it could
have been. In fact, a popular Egyptian Muslim preacher
has commented that fourteen hundred years ago Islam
gave women rights that are being ignored today.

They're being ignored because the factors that affect
Muslim societies—poverty, illiteracy, and no access to
education—all negatively affect women's rights. But they're
also being ignored because people follow cultural practices
and mistakenly think they're religious practices. That's why
a big part of promoting women's rights requires educating
people about the difference between religion and culture.

We hear a great deal about the difficulties Muslim
women face. Yet the many Muslim women who are *not*
oppressed are rarely mentioned on the airwaves. So let's
take a minute to talk about them as well.

The four largest Muslim populations on earth are
those in Indonesia, Pakistan, India, and Bangladesh; each
of these countries has had a woman president or prime
minister.[11] In fact, at least *six* Muslim women have been
presidents or prime ministers of five Muslim-majority
countries (Pakistan, Indonesia, Bangladesh, Kosovo, and
Turkey) in modern times. That's not counting the current
Muslim queens or the Muslim queens and rulers of the
past. Not only did these Muslim women presidents and
prime ministers have the resources and personal abilities
to rise to such high government office, but the Muslim
populations of these countries supported their rise.

Muslim women, like women of other religious groups, come from all types of backgrounds and do all kinds of jobs. Some are doctors, professors, lawyers, and politicians. In Egypt, one-third of the technical and professional workforce consists of women, the same portion as in South Korea.[12] Muslim women are or have been government officials or members of parliament in numerous countries, including Turkey, Kenya, the United Kingdom, Nigeria, Iran, Morocco, Malaysia, India, Indonesia, Egypt, Bangladesh, and Pakistan.

Both Iran and the United Arab Emirates are Muslim-majority countries, and in both countries more women than men attend universities. Over half of Iranian women have postsecondary (college) educations. Women in the United Arab Emirates are also being trained as muftis, or Islamic religious scholars. Women in Morocco, as well, are being trained as religious scholars. Iranian women include judges, lawyers, governors, doctors, and a winner of the Nobel Prize (Shirin Ebadi).

In Yemen, one of the Arab world's poorest countries, many Muslim women are working for greater rights and freedom. They are making progress. For years, Muslim women lawyers, journalists, and activists worked hard, alongside religious scholars, to eliminate child marriage; in 2009, the Yemeni parliament finally approved establishing a minimum marriage age of seventeen for both boys and girls. Marriage age continues to be a controversial issue in Yemen, because the country is so poor that families see early marriage for their girls as a way to provide for their future. One Yemeni Muslim woman activist who has long championed nonviolent struggle to increase women's safety and rights is Tawakul Karmam, one of the youngest winners of the Nobel Peace Prize. In Saudi Arabia, conservative tribal culture does discriminate against women. But even so, many Saudi women are educated professionals. According to recent data from Gallup, the ratio of women to men enrolled in secondary education in Saudi Arabia is nine to ten. That's nearly equal, and the number is increasing. It's a greater proportion of women enrolled in secondary education than in, for example, India. The Gallup poll found that thirty-two percent of Saudi women have postsecondary educations.[13]

Thousands of Muslims and Islamic scholars today are working to eliminate oppressive cultural traditions. They are also working to modernize the condition of Muslim countries. When that happens, the condition of women will improve.

## Where We're Going: Reforms and Modernization

Most women in Muslim-majority countries do want equal rights with men. More than that, a recent world poll conducted by Gallup found that, in most countries, majorities of Muslim men, too, want to improve the rights of women.[14] Interestingly, according to this poll, Muslim men's approval of women's rights did not depend upon whether the men were "secular" or "religious." In fact, in Lebanon, Morocco, and Iran, Muslim men who supported women's rights were found to be *more* religious than those Muslim men who did not support women's rights.[15]

Like all ancient religions, Islam is largely about justice and universal values. But, also like other ancient religions, parts of the fiqh contain rules that were typical of the world a thousand years ago, but that aren't suitable for today's world. Some of the fiqh relates to historical circumstances that have long since disappeared. Many Muslim scholars today, both men and women, are reevaluating and modernizing these aspects of the fiqh.

Muslim women's movements, in particular, have been growing. Although some Muslim women were religious scholars even in early Islam, traditional Islamic law was developed by men. Muslim women scholars today are addressing that omission by reinterpreting the Qur'an and the Sunnah.

"We think medieval male cultural norms got in the way of the development of our religion," many Muslim women scholars have been asserting. "We want to reinterpret the Qur'an and the Sunnah *without* medieval male attitudes."

Modernization takes time. It's particularly difficult in poor and war-torn countries, like Afghanistan. But I am optimistic that it will happen.

## Conclusion

Nearly a thousand years ago, some Islamic scholars wrote that the true abode of Islam was not a particular territory ruled by Muslims, but any place where Muslims could freely and openly practice their religion.[16] I feel lucky to be an American Muslim; I am free, under my country's laws, to practice my religion.

I believe that the United States, perhaps more than any other country in the world, is compatible with Islam, because it values religious freedom and multicultural respect. The Qur'an values religious freedom, too, in the verses forbidding forced conversion. It also values pluralism, as it says, "[God] made you into different nations and tribes so you could learn from one another"[17] and "Among the signs of God . . . is the diversity of your languages and colors."[18]

I am proud to be Muslim and American. Islam is one of many American religions. It is my hope that my fellow Americans will increasingly accept it as such.

# Notes

## Chapter 4: Fasting

1. Sunset is when Sunni Muslims break their fasts. Shi'i Muslims break their fasts a little later, at dusk, when the sky is almost dark. Sunni and Shi'a ("Shi'i" is the adjective form) are discussed more thoroughly in Chapter 15.
2. Mike Sando, "Keeping the Faith," ESPN, http://espn.go.com /blog/nfcwest/post/_/id/22823/video-keeping-the-faith and youtube .com/watch?v=DhjsQzw_lGo.
3. These dates can vary by a day or two; the reason is discussed later in the chapter.
4. From John Feeney, "Ramadan's Lanterns," *Saudi Aramco World Magazine*, March/April 1992, p. 14. For the online version, see saudiaramcoworld.com/issue/199202/ramadan.s.lanterns.htm.
5. Ibid.

## Chapter 5: Holidays

1. "Bean Pie, My Brother?" National Public Radio, September 10, 2010, at npr.org/templates/story/story.php?storyId=129778278.
2. "CE" stands for "Common Era" and is used in place of "AD," or *anno Domini*, which means "in the year of our Lord," referring to Christ.
3. BBC News, "Afghans Donate Blood for Ashura," January 9, 2009.

## Chapter 6: Donating to Charity

1. Adapted from Sarah Conover and Freda Crane, *Ayat Jamilah: Beautiful Signs: A Treasury of Islamic Wisdom for Children and Parents* (Spokane: Eastern Washington University Press, 2004), pp. 16–18.

## Chapter 7: A Muslim Pilgrim's Progress

1. See www.census.gov for the populations of American cities.

## Chapter 8: Everyday Rules of Behavior for Muslims

1. Surah 22, verse 30.
2. Surah 2, verse 42.
3. Surah 45, verse 7.
4. Adapted from Sarah Conover and Freda Crane, *Ayat Jamilah: Beautiful Signs: A Treasury of Islamic Wisdom for Children and Parents* (Spokane: Eastern Washington University Press, 2004), pp. 114–16.
5. Surah 49, verse 12.
6. You can find these commands in the following verses: Surah 28, verse 77; Surah 3, verse 200; Surah 5, verse 8, Surah 5, verse 1.
7. What not to do can be found in Surah 49, verse 11, and Surah 31, verse 18.
8. Surah 3, verse 134.
9. Surah 41, verse 46.
10. Surah 15, verse 85.
11. This version is adapted from Conover and Crane, *Ayat Jamilah: Beautiful Signs,* p. 73.
12. Surah 49, verse 11.

## Chapter 9: Fashion Sense

1. Gamal el-Banna, quoted in Pamela Taylor, "A Modern Muslim" in *Pakistan Voice,* September 25, 2010, at pakistanvoice.net/?p=1090.
2. timesonline.co.uk/tol/news/world/middle_east/article3499122.ece.
3. Khaled Abou el Fadl, "Hijab: The Issue and the Evidence" at scholarofthehouse.org/lecturetapes.html and *Conference of the Books,* pp. 291–96
4. "Islam and the Media," on *Forum,* KQED radio, April 29, 1999.

## Chapter 11: Muhammad and His Mission

1. Surah 96, verses 1–5.
2. Huston Smith, *The World's Religions: Our Great Wisdom Traditions* (San Francisco: HarperSanFrancisco, 1991), p. 256, quoting Ameer Ali, *The Spirit of Islam.*

## Chapter 12: How Muslims View the World

1. Surah 19, verse 21.
2. Surah 20, verse 120.
3. Surah 2, verse 62.
4. In 2009, 45 percent of American Muslims believed in evolution and 48 percent of all Americans believed in evolution. See pewforum.org /Science-and-Bioethics/Religious-Differences-on-the-Question -of-Evolution.aspx.

## Chapter 13: The Basis of Islam

1. Akbar S. Ahmed, *Islam Today* (London: I. B. Tauris, 1999), pp. 28–29.
2. See, e.g., Ephesians 6: 5–9, Exodus 21: 26–27, and Titus 2: 9–10.

## Chapter 14: From Sand Dunes to Spain

1. Arthur Goldschmidt Jr., *A Concise History of the Middle East,* 7th ed. (Boulder, CO: Westview Press, 2002), p. 54.
2. Surah 2, verse 256.
3. Surah 109, verse 6.
4. Surah 10, verse 99.
5. Asma Afsaruddin, *The First Muslims: History and Memory* (Oxford: Oneworld, 2008), p. 42.
6. Ibrahim al-Kadi, "Origins of Cryptology: The Arab Contributions" in *Selections from Cryptologia: History, People, and Technology* (Boston: Artech House, 1998), ed. C. A. Deavours et al., pp. 98–99. The Arabic numeral system, including the zero, was developed in India; Arabs recognized its value and put it into widespread circulation.
7. Simon Singh, *The Code Book: The Science of Secrecy from Ancient Egypt to Quantum Cryptography* (New York: 1999; Anchor Books, 2000), pp. 14–17.

8. Jonathan Bloom and Sheila Blair, *Islam: A Thousand Years of Faith and Power* (New Haven: Yale University Press, 2002), pp. 131–32.
9. Ibrahim al-Kadi, "Origins of Cryptology," p. 116.
10. Khaled Abou El Fadl, *The Place of Tolerance in Islam,* ed. Joshua Cohen and Ian Lague for *Boston Review* (Boston: Beacon Press, 2002), p. 19.
11. Afsaruddin, *The First Muslims*, p. 7.
12. Ibid., pp. 7–8.
13. Surah 2, verse 190.
14. Ibid.
15. Surah 8, verse 61.
16. Surah 4, verse 90.

## Chapter 15: Who's Who

1. Clifton E. Marsh, *The Lost-Found Nation of Islam in America* (Maryland: Scarecrow Press, 1996; rpt., 2000), p. 61.

## Chapter 16: Muslims

1. Louis Werner, "Mushaira: Pakistan's Festival of Poetry," *Saudi Aramco World* 59, no. 5 (September/October 2008), p. 26.
2. Lark Ellen Gould, "A Nation of Bards," *Saudi Aramco World* 39, no. 6 (November/December 1988).
3. See, e.g., James Brook, "Honor Killings of Wives Is Outlawed in Brazil," *New York Times,* March 29, 1991.
4. John Feffer, "The Politics Behind Misunderstanding Islam," cbsnews.com/stories/2010/11/07/opinion/main7033060.shtml.
5. A minority of American Muslims attend mosques, with some estimates as low as 7 percent (csmonitor.com/2004/0421/p09s02-coop .html) and some as high as 40 percent (Gallup).
6. Mohamed Younis, "Muslim Americans Exemplify Diversity, Potential: Key Findings from a New Report by the Gallup Center for Muslim Studies," gallup.com/poll/116260/muslim-americans -exemplify-diversity-potential.aspx, March 2, 2009.
7. See pewresearch.org/pubs/483/muslim-americans.
8. Ibid.
9. Ibid.

10. See  gallup.com/poll/116260/muslim-americans-exemplify-diversity
   -potential.aspx.

11. India's prime minister was Hindu, not Muslim, but she was elected
   in a country with a huge Muslim population.

12. John L. Esposito and Dalia Mogahed, *Who Speaks for Islam?: What
   a Billion Muslims Really Think* (New York: Gallup Press, 2007),
   p. 102.

13. Ibid., p. 104.

14. Ibid., p. 121.

15. Ibid., p. 123.

16. Khaled Abou El Fadl, *The Great Theft: Wrestling Islam from the Extremists* (New York: HarperSanFrancisco, 2005), p. 228.

17. Surah 49, verse 13.

18. Surah 30, verse 22.

# Bibliography

## Books

Abou El Fadl, Khaled. *Conference of the Books: The Search for Beauty in Islam*. Lanham, MD: University Press of America, 2001.

———. *The Great Theft: Wrestling Islam from the Extremists*. San Francisco: HarperSanFrancisco, 2005.

———. *The Place of Tolerance in Islam*. Boston: Beacon Press, 2002.

Afsaruddin, Asma. *The First Muslims: History and Memory*. Oxford: Oneworld, 2008.

Ahmed, Akbar S. *Islam Today*. London: I. B. Tauris, 1999.

Ali, Ahmed. *Al-Qur'an: A Contemporary Translation*. Princeton: Princeton University Press, 2001.

Ali-Karamali, Sumbul. *The Muslim Next Door: The Qur'an, the Media, and that Veil Thing*. Ashland, OR: White Cloud Press, 2008.

Arberry, A. J. *The Koran Interpreted*. New York: Touchstone, 1996. First published 1955 by Allen & Unwin Ltd.

Asad, Muhammad. *The Message of the Qur'an*. Gibraltar: Dar al-Andalus, 1980.

Barlas, Asma. *"Believing Women" in Islam: Unreading Patriarchal Interpretations of the Qur'an*. Austin: University of Texas Press, 2002.

Bassiouni, M. Cherif, ed. *The Islamic Criminal Justice System*. New York: Oceana, 1982.

Bloom, Jonathan, and Sheila Blair. *Islam: A Thousand Years of Faith and Power*. New Haven: Yale University Press, 2002.

Cleary, Thomas. *The Essential Koran: The Heart of Islam*. New York: HarperCollins, 1994.

Conover, Sarah, and Freda Crane. *Ayat Jamilah: Beautiful Signs: A Treasure of Islamic Wisdom for Children and Parents.* Spokane: Eastern Washington University Press, 2004.

Curiel, Jonathan. *Al-America: Travels Through America's Arab and Islamic Roots.* New York: The New Press, 2008.

Daniel, Norman. *Islam and the West: The Making of an Image.* Oxford: Oneworld, 2000.

Denny, Frederick Mathewson. *An Introduction to Islam.* New York: Macmillan, 1994.

Esposito, John and Dalia Mogahed. *Who Speaks for Islam: What a Billion Muslims Really Think.* New York: Gallup, 2007.

Esposito, John L. *Islam: The Straight Path.* New York: Oxford University Press, 3rd ed., 1998.

———. *Islam and Politics.* Syracuse: Syracuse University Press, 1998.

———. *The Islamic Threat: Myth or Reality?* New York: Oxford University Press, 1992.

———. *What Everyone Needs to Know About Islam.* New York: Oxford University Press, 2002.

Esposito, John L., and Natana DeLong-Bas. *Women in Muslim Family Law.* Syracuse: Syracuse University Press, 2001.

Fluehr-Lobban, Carolyn. *Islamic Society in Practice.* Gainesville: University of Florida Press, 1994.

al-Gailani, Noorah, and Chris Smith. *The Islamic Year: Suras, Stories, and Celebrations.* Gloucestershire: Hawthorn Press, 2002.

Gibb, H. A. R. *Mohammedanism: An Historical Survey,* 2nd ed. London: Oxford University Press, 1969.

Goldschmidt, Arthur Jr. *A Concise History of the Middle East.* 7th ed. Boulder, CO: Westview Press, 2002.

Hawting, Gerald. *The First Dynasty of Islam: The Umayyad Caliphate AD 661–750.* 2nd ed. London: Rutledge, 2000.

Hecker, Eugene A. *A Short History of Women's Rights.* Westport: Greenwood Press, 1914.

Hoppen, K. Theodore. *The Mid-Victorian Generation: 1846–1886.* Oxford: Clarendon Press, 1998.

Hourani, Albert. *A History of the Arab Peoples.* Cambridge: Belknap Press of Harvard University Press, 1991.

Hufton, Olwen. *The Prospect Before Her.* New York: Vintage Books, 1998.

Humphreys, Stephen. *Between Memory and Desire: The Middle East in a Troubled Age.* Berkeley: University of California Press, 2005.

Johnson, James Turner. *The Holy War Idea in Western and Islamic Traditions.* University Park: Pennsylvania State University Press, 1997.

al-Kadi, Ibrahim. "Origins of Cryptology: The Arab Contributions." In *Selections from Cryptologia,* edited by C.A. Deavours. Boston: Artech House, 1998.

Katz, Victor J. *A History of Mathematics.* New York: HarperCollins, 1993.

Kennedy, Hugh. *The Prophet and the Age of the Caliphates: The Islamic Near East from the Sixth to the Eleventh Century.* New York: Longman, 1991.

Khadduri, Majid. *War and Peace in the Law of Islam.* Baltimore: Johns Hopkins University Press, 1955.

Kolchin, Peter. *American Slavery 1619–1877.* New York: Hill and Wang, 1993.

Kurzman, Charles, ed. *Liberal Islam: A Sourcebook.* New York: Oxford University Press, 1998.

Malcolm, Noel. *Bosnia: A Short History.* London: MacMillan, 1994.

Mallat, Chibli. *Introduction to Middle Eastern Law.* New York: Oxford University Press, 2007.

Marsh, Clifton E. *The Lost-Found Nation of Islam in America.* Lanham, MD: Scarecrow Press, 2000.

Menocal, Maria Rosa. *The Ornament of the World: How Muslims, Jews, and Christians Created a Culture of Tolerance in Medieval Spain.* New York: Little, Brown, and Company, 2002.

Mernissi, Fatima. *The Forgotten Queens of Islam.* Translated by Mary Jo Lakeland. Cambridge: Polity Press, 1993.

———. *The Veil and the Male Elite.* Translated by Mary Jo Lakeland. New York: Addison-Wesley, 1991.

Morgan, Michael Hamilton. *Lost History: The Enduring Legacy of Muslim Scientists, Thinkers, and Artists.* Washington, D.C.: National Geographic Society, 2007.

an-Naim, Abdullahi Ahmed. *Toward an Islamic Reformation: Civil Liberties, Human Rights, and International Law.* New York: Syracuse, 1990.

Nasr, Seyyed Hossein. *Ideals and Realities of Islam.* Chicago: ABC International Group, 2000.

Parrinder, Geoffrey. *Jesus in the Qur'an.* Oxford: Oneworld, 1965.

———. *Mysticism in the World's Religions.* Oxford: Oneworld, 1996.

Peters, F. E. *A Reader on Classical Islam.* Princeton: Princeton University Press, 1994.

Peters, Rudolph. *Jihad in Classical and Modern Islam.* Princeton: Marcus Weiner Publishers, 1996.

Rahman, Fazlur. *Major Themes of the Qur'an.* Minneapolis: Bibliotheca Islamica, 1994.

Rippin, Andrew. *Muslims: Their Religious Beliefs and Practices.* London: Routledge, 1990.

Said, Edward. *Covering Islam: How the Media and the Experts Determine How We See the Rest of the World.* Rev. ed. New York: Vintage, 1997.

———. *Orientalism.* New York: Penguin, 1991. First published in 1978 by Routledge & Kegan Paul Ltd.

Schacht, Joseph. *An Introduction to Islamic Law.* Oxford: Clarendon Press, 1991. First published 1964 by Oxford University Press.

Schmidt, Alvin J. *Veiled and Silenced: How Culture Shaped Sexist Theology.* Macon, GA: Mercer University Press, 1989.

Schulze, Reinhard. *A Modern History of the Islamic World.* New York: I. B. Tauris, 2000. First published 1995 by C. H. Beck'sche Verlagsbuchhandlung.

Sells, Michael. *Approaching the Qur'an: The Early Revelations.* Ashland, OR: White Cloud Press, 1999.

———. *Stations of Desire: Love Elegies from Ibn Arabi and New Poems.* Jerusalem: Ibis Editions, 2004.

Shah, Idries. *The Sufis.* New York: Doubleday, 1964.

Singh, Simon. *The Code Book: The Science of Secrecy from Ancient Egypt to Quantum Cryptography.* New York: Anchor, 2000.

Smith, Huston. *The World's Religions: Our Great Wisdom Traditions.* San Francisco: HarperSanFrancisco, 1991.

Smith, Jane I. *Islam in America*. New York: Columbia University Press, 1999.

Trevelyan, G. M. *English Social History: A Survey of Six Centuries, Chaucer to Queen Victoria*. Harmondsworth, UK: Penguin, 1967. First published 1946 by Longmans, Green and Co.

Wadud, Amina. *Inside the Gender Jihad: Women's Reform in Islam*. Oxford: Oneworld, 2006.

———. *Qur'an and Woman: Rereading the Sacred Text from a Woman's Perspective*. New York: Oxford University Press, 1999.

Williams, John Alden. *The Word of Islam*. Austin: University of Texas Press, 1994.

### Articles

Abou El Fadl, Khaled. "Fatwa on Women Leading Prayer," at *Scholar of the House*, http://scholarofthehouse.stores.yahoo.net/onwolepr.html.

———. "Islam and the Challenge of Democracy," *Boston Review: A Political and Literary Forum*, April/May 2003, http://bostonreview.net/BR28.2/abou.html.

———. "Terrorism Is at Odds with Islamic Tradition," *Los Angeles Times*, August 22, 2001, http://articles.latimes.com/2001/aug/22/local/me-36804.

BBC News. "Afghans Donate Blood for Ashura," 9 January 2009, http://news.bbc.co.uk/2/hi/7820746.stm.

Feeney, John. "Ramadan's Lanterns," *Saudi Aramco World Magazine*, March/April 1992, 15–23.

Ferguson, Barbara. "Woman Imam Raises Mixed Emotions," *Arab News*, March 20, 2005, http://www.arabnews.com/?page=4&section=0&article=60721&d=20&m=3&y=2005.

Goldberg, Kate. "Islam Hijacked by Terror," *BBC News*, October 11, 2001, http://news.bbc.co.uk/2/hi/americas/1591024.stm.

Gould, Lark Ellen. "A Nation of Bards," *Saudi Aramco World* 39, no. 6, November/December 1988, 32–36.

Harrison, Frances. "Women Graduates Challenge Iran," *BBC News*, September 19, 2006, http://news.bbc.co.uk/go/pr/fr/-/2/hi/middle_east/5359672.stm.

Muir, Jim. "Iran Condemns Attacks on U.S.," *BBC News,* September 17, 2001, news.bbc.co.uk/2/hi/middle_east/1549573.stm.

Sachs, Susan. "In Iran, More Women Leaving Nest for University," *The New York Times,* July 22, 2000, nytimes.com/2000/07/22 /world/in-iran-more-women-leaving-nest-for-university.html? pagewanted=all&src=pm.

Werner, Louis. "Mushaira: Pakistan's Festival of Poetry," *Saudi Aramco World* 59, no. 5, September/October 2008, 24–33.

## Select Dictionaries and Encyclopedias

*The New Encyclopedia of Islam.* Cyril Glassé, ed. Walnut Creek, Calif.: Alta Mira Press, 1989; rev. ed., 2001.

*The Oxford Dictionary of Islam.* John L. Esposito, ed. Oxford, 2003.

*The Oxford Encyclopedia of the Modern Islamic World.* John L. Esposito, ed. Oxford, 1995.

*The Oxford History of Islam.* John L. Esposito, ed. Oxford, 1999.

## Other Sources

Allit, Patrick. *Victorian Britain, Part I,* course guidebook and lecture recording. The Teaching Company Limited Partnership, 2002.

"Bean Pie, My Brother?" National Public Radio, September 10, 2010, npr.org/templates/story/story.php?storyId=129778278.

The Council on American-Islamic Relations. "Islamic Statements Against Terrorism in the Wake of the September 11 Mass Murders," www.cair.com/AmericanMuslims/AntiTerrorism/IslamicState mentsAgainstTerrorism.aspx.

Kurzman, Charles. "Islamic Statements Against Terrorism," unc .edu/~kurzman/terror.htm.

Lubin, Tim. "Islamic Responses to the Sept. 11 Attack," http://home .wlu.edu/~lubint/islamonWTC.htm.

Safi, Omid. "Scholars of Islam & the Tragedy of September 11th," http://groups.colgate.edu/aarislam/response.htm.

# Index

## About the Author

Sumbul Ali-Karamali holds a BA from Stanford University and a JD from the University of California, Davis. She earned a graduate degree in Islamic law from the University of London's School of Oriental and African studies, where she also served as a teaching assistant in Islamic law. She has been a research associate at the Centre of Islamic and Middle Eastern Law in London and is the author of the highly praised and award-winning adult book *The Muslim Next Door: the Qur'an, the Media, and that Veil Thing.*